MW00784812

"*A Decision to Love* addresses the topics all marriage preparation programs consider, but it does so in a crisp and focused way. It challenges engaged couples to move beyond their typical romantic images and polite conversations about love and marriage. It isn't afraid to ask tough questions and to call couples to some straight talk on issues such as the meaning of commitment, the influence of significant family members, and patterns and signs of addictive behavior, as well as their experience of God, faith, and religion.

"I particularly liked the Information Boxes, a series of remarkably clear and succinct treatments of key issues dispersed throughout the text. Topics include cohabitation, AIDS, spouse abuse, premarital counseling, co-dependency, dual-career couples, and interfaith marriages. These brief summaries will provide rich material for the staff as well as for the engaged couples."

Rev. Thomas L. Boland
Past President, National Association of Catholic Family Life Ministers

"I find *A Decision to Love* to be excellent overall....The inclusion of explanations of terms alongside their mention in the text strengthens the presentation....The 'family of origin' and the 'sexuality' sections are especially outstanding....This marriage preparation manual is very well done. Congratulations to the authors and the publisher."

Rev. Richard J. Garcia
Past National Executive Priest, Catholic Engaged Encounter USA

"One more marriage preparation program has reached my desk. Ho hum.

"Except that *A Decision to Love* offers the freshest, most creative, and contemporary approach I've seen in years. Authored by John and Susan Vollmer Midgley, published by Twenty-Third Publications, *Decision*...features a simply and personally written couple's manual, a helpful guide for liturgy planning, and a workbook to assist parish leaders in the preparation process.

"The manual will give engaged couples both theoretical and practical knowledge about communication, fighting, finances, children, spirituality, and—most notably—an understanding of family of origin, on the impact of personality, and of sexuality without stereotype. Also beneficial are the many capsule 'thought-provokers' on such topics as pre-nuptial agreements, co-dependency, spouse abuse, AIDS, sexual addiction, infertility, dual careers, and being 'Mr. Mom.'

"But couples will benefit most from 'His Page' and 'Her Page,' worksheets with questions that will provoke insight and, if the couple allows it, very helpful confrontation. The leader's manual describes one-day and three-evening formats for using *A Decision to Love* in groups, fresh and enjoyable ice-breakers, brief talk outlines, and excellent background material especially on family systems.

"*A Decision to Love* is the best marriage preparation program I've seen in twenty years!"

Valerie Dillon
Past President, National Family Life Directors
Author, *Becoming a Woman*

"*A Decision to Love* is a first-rate resource fir use with virtually any marriage preparation program, whether a single-session model, a series of evenings, or a weekend. John and Susan include resource and discussion materials on every key aspect of marriage, and their insights on how to present the content in ways suitable for engaged couples is right on the money. Any engaged couple who uses this material will be fortunate, indeed."

Mitch Finley
Author, *Married Love: A Special Way of Being Alive*

"*A Decision to Love* manages to put into perspective a fact often overlooked by engaged couples: the wedding is one day in our lives, the honeymoon, perhaps a week. Engagement is not a preparation for that brief period; it is a time to prepare for the rest of our lives.

"In the hands of a skillful leader, this program will give a loving relationship the tools needed for survival. After thirty-eight years of my own marriage, we are just beginning to discover many of the issues raised in this thoughtful and well-written book. All couples—engaged, newly married, and not so newly married—will find food for thought, topics for discussion, and issues still needing clarification in the helpful workbook sections.

"This is excellent—an answer to prayer for many parishes."

Kathleen Chesto
Author, *Family Spirituality*

"John and Susan Vollmer Midgley bring their considerable pastoral experience and personal insights to the task of marriage preparation in this new book. They confront the major issues of the day (substance abuse, AIDS, dual-career couples) as they invite engaged couples to discuss honestly the many aspects of married life. *A Decision to Love* will be a valuable resource to parishes in their ministry with engaged couples."

Paul Covino
Co-author, *Celebrating Marriage*

"What a joy to discover *A Decision to Love*. There lies in these pages a carefully crafted resource and communication tool ideal for marriage preparation, but also valuable for many years into marriage. This gem is packed with timely information, designed to be practical. The layout and exercises are highly conducive to communicating, listening, sharing. There is a sensitive and caring spirit pervading this work of love, giving it a spiritual yet practical flavor that very much resembles marriage itself. All who use this material are likely to find direction and wisdom in their love's journey."

Lawrence J. Losoncy, Ph.D.
Licensed Marriage-Family Therapist

A marriage preparation program

A Decision *to* Love

[LEADER'S GUIDE]

JOHN M. V. MIDGLEY and
SUSAN VOLLMER MIDGLEY

TWENTY-THIRD PUBLICATIONS
twentythirdpublications.com

Excerpts from the *Lectionary for Mass for Use in the Dioceses of the United States, second edition* Copyright ©1970, 1986, 1992, 1998, 2001 Confraternity of Christian Doctrine, Inc., Washington, D.C. All rights reserved. No part of this work may be reproduced or transmitted in any form or by any means, electronic or mechanical, including photocopying, recording, or by any information storage and retrieval system, without permission in writing from the copyright owner.

The Revised Grail Psalms Copyright © 2010, Conception Abbey/The Grail, admin. by GIA Publications, Inc., www.giamusic.com All rights reserved.

The English translation of some Psalm responses, some Alleluia and Gospel verses, some Summaries, and the Titles and Conclusion of the Readings, from the *Lectionary for Mass* © 1968, 1981, 1997, International Committee on English in the Liturgy, Inc., Washington, D.C. All rights reserved.

Excerpts from the English translation of *The Order of Celebrating Matrimony* © 2013, International Commission on English in the Liturgy Corporation (ICEL); the English translation of Psalm Responses, Alleluia Verses from *Lectionary for Mass* © 1969, 1981, 1997, ICEL; excerpts from the English translation of *The Roman Missal* © 2010, ICEL. All rights reserved.

Texts contained in this work derived whole or in part from liturgical texts copyrighted by the International Commission on English in the Liturgy (ICEL) have been published here with the confirmation of the Committee on Divine Worship, United States Conference of Catholic Bishops. No other texts in this work have been formally reviewed or approved by the United States Conference of Catholic Bishops.

"The Johns Hopkins Twenty Questions: Are You an Alcoholic?"
Courtesy of Johns Hopkins University Hospital. Used with permission.

"Two Different Directions" by John Denver. © 1991 Cherry Mountain Music.
All rights reserved. Used by permission.

Traits of a Healthy Family. © 1983 by Dolores Curran. Courtesy of HarperSanFrancisco. Used with permission.

TWENTY-THIRD PUBLICATIONS
One Montauk Avenue, Suite 200
New London, CT 06320
(860) 437-3012 or (800) 321-0411
www.twentythirdpublications.com

© Copyright 1992, 2000, 2009, 2016 John M.V. Midgley and Susan Vollmer Midgley. All rights reserved.
No part of this publication may be reproduced in any manner without prior written permission
of the publisher. Write to Permissions Editor.

ISBN 978-1-62785-236-4
Library of Congress Catalog Card Number 2016952858
Printed in the U.S.A

 A division of Bayard, Inc.

Contents

Information Boxes

(page numbers refer to the pages in the Couple's Book)

A Decision
to Love

Introduction

Welcome to the leader's guide of *A Decision to Love*. Because you are part of a marriage preparation team, you have a deep concern for the health and well-being of the engaged couple's future marriage. You are investing your time, talent, and emotional and psychological energy into this. It's a big investment, but the returns are priceless.

You will find that being part of a marriage preparation process can be exciting, stimulating, beautiful, exhausting, frustrating, and scary. It's exciting to observe a young couple discover something new about themselves. It's stimulating to your own relationships to have other married couples give talks on communication skills and other topics. It's beautiful to have an engaged couple thank you at the end of a program for what you've done for them. It's exhausting to have to leave home on an evening or weekend, arrange for a sitter, rush off to church at the end of a long day to be with couples who may not want to be there in the first place. It's frustrating when the program doesn't run as well as you think it should. And it's scary to see what impact your words may have on the engaged couples who hear them.

A Decision to Love

This workbook is entitled *A Decision to Love* be-cause we believe that loving and being loved is a decision. Real love is not something that just happens once and never changes. Rather, because we are always growing and changing, our love has to grow and change. Keeping that love alive and renewed demands much from us: First, it demands a commitment to our love; second, it demands a belief that the love is worthwhile; and finally, it demands a decision to continue loving, even when we may not feel lovable or may not feel like loving anyone.

God's decision to create, sustain, and love us is the model of all love, which is to love unconditionally and fully. Jesus is our model in this; he walked among us, and taught us through his example about love. As married couples, we are called to this kind of love and to this kind of decision. Jesus' life and love have challenged us to learn to give love to our partners with the fullness and depth that we are loved by God.

Leader's Guide

This leader's guide that accompanies the engaged couple's edition is meant to assist you in running a marriage preparation program. It includes (in reduced form) all the pages found in the engaged couple's book as well as further suggestions on running a program. It also contains exercises that are not in the couple's edition. Since this edition is also meant to be a planning guide, we have included notes to assist you with the planning of your marriage preparation program.

Purpose of Marriage Preparation

Why have you volunteered to help couples prepare for their marriage? Your answer to this question will be personal, but it has to include the fact that the overall purpose for marriage preparation is to help couples prepare for a marital relationship that will be a life-giving journey of love, hope, and faith. As the title of this workbook indicates, we believe marriage is based on a decision that a couple makes to love each other. This decision is not made once and for all, but is an on-going, growing, and maturing decision that has to be reaffirmed every day in the couple's life together.

Engaged couples typically are so romantically "in love" with each other that they are not initially receptive to the idea of love as a decision. They may think it just "happens" to them. They see love purely as an emotion, which at this time in their lives is overflowing. In this workbook we attempt to affirm this, but also to encourage them to move beyond that stage and mature in their love.

Flexibility of Workbook

A Decision to Love is designed to fit into any new or existing marriage preparation program. It is not designed as an entire program in itself; thus it allows you greater flexibility to meet the needs of the program that you may already be running in your parish or diocese. Later in this volume, for those who are just beginning a program or looking for new ideas in an existing one, we suggest ways to run a marriage preparation program.

If you decide to use *A Decision to Love* in your already existing program, we suggest that you carefully select from it the chapters and the material in each chapter that you intend to use in your program. There are in this book eight chapters, a wedding liturgy planning section, information boxes of useful information, and a resource appendix that cover much more material than the typical marriage preparation program allows for. Encourage your engaged couples

to complete, on their own at a later time, whatever material you do not cover in your program.

His Pages and Her Pages

In all the chapters of *A Decision to Love*, you will find a His Page and a Her Page, with the same questions in each. Allow enough time for each person to answer the questions on his or her page and to discuss their answers together. These pages should be removed from the couple's book to allow each the opportunity to answer the questions privately. The couple should then confer with each other, comparing their answers.

Some questions are open-ended, requiring answers of some length; some are closed-ended, requiring short answers: multiple choice, true or false, and fill-ins. This variety is intentional, since every individual will prefer one style over another. Marriage preparation coordinators across the country have reported that people in marriage preparation programs are about evenly divided in their preference.

If the amount of time available during your program is a concern, consider assigning only the short-answer and multiple choice questions to the couples. They should be encouraged, however, to answer the remaining questions later on their own.

Case Studies and Group Discussions

You will find various group questions and case studies throughout *A Decision to Love*, including several "baby cases" in Chapter 6. We have found case studies to be useful in small group discussions. If you decide to use the material in this way, here are a few suggestions.

First, in leading a small group discussion on a case study, the golden rule is that there are no wrong answers. A good case study is open to interpretation, analysis, and an exchange of opinions. Correcting someone when he or she expresses an opinion will discourage any further desire to share an opinion. Allow a free flow of possibilities for each case study. If your small group seems to reach a premature "solution," they should be challenged to look at other possibilities.

Another point to remember in your small group discussions is that no one should ever be pressured into saying something. You can encourage a quiet individual to speak by a friendly glance or nod. Or you may ask a non-threatening, open-ended question in order to elicit some response. In any event, respect their desire to be silent, if that is their choice.

Questionnaires and Exercises

There are various questionnaires, exercises, and ice-breakers found in the couple's edition and this leader's edition. Chapters 2, 3, and 4 in particular offer a variety of resources you can offer the couples in your program.

Information Boxes

A feature of *A Decision to Love* is the many information boxes found throughout the book, featuring topics such as cohabitation, AIDS, pre-marital counseling, dual-career couples, interfaith marriages, co-dependency, alcoholism and addictions, fighting, in-laws, remarriage, divorce, jealousy, spouse abuse, living with parents and natural family planning. These brief information boxes may serve as discussion starters, thought provokers, and supplemental aides to presentations given in your marriage preparation program. The table of contents lists all of these boxes and the page where each one may be found.

Issues of Special Focus

In the couple's edition you will also find boxes with questions targeted for couples with special issues to deal with, such as pregnancy, previous marriage, stepchildren, significant age difference, and older couples. There is no specific space given in the workbook for writing answers to these special focus questions. During your program, encourage the engaged to read these questions and, during the breaks or on their own time, discuss any that may pertain to them.

Relationship Check

Each chapter ends with a relationship check. It is important for engaged couples to get an over-all assessment of how they feel after each chapter's topic. Stress the importance of this exercise. Couples are often amazed that after a certain topic is covered, one of the two of them may not be comfortable with their answers and discussions and may want to pursue the subject further. A glance back over the chap-

ters at the end of the program will highlight for the engaged couples the topics that may still need work.

Planning of the Wedding Liturgy

A section on planning the wedding liturgy is also included in the couple's edition. If time and interest allow, it is often a good idea to go through this with the engaged couples. Most of them have never participated in planning a liturgy before, and they may be feeling somewhat lost and overwhelmed at this time. This is a good opportunity for you to get couples thinking about their wedding day and how their liturgy will be a symbol, an expression, of their Christian marriage.

All prayers, responses, and reading options for the ceremony are presented in the planning section, including two copies of the Planning Sheet (a draft copy and a final copy) so the couple can prepare a final list of all the decisions they make regarding their wedding ceremony.

Resource Appendix

The last information found in this workbook is an extensive listing of self-help and referral resources. During an encounter such as a marriage preparation program, some individuals will come upon personal issues in their lives that they may want assistance dealing with. This resource list offers national 800, or hotline, numbers, addresses, and Web sites of groups they may be interested in. If you observe that a couple appears unusually troubled by a presentation or exercise, you may want to simply ask if everything is all right and make yourself available to them before or after the program or during breaks. If it's appropriate, you may wish to refer them to a professional. No marriage preparation team couple is ever asked to take on a role they are not qualified to assume. We also recommend that you have local numbers for these groups or for professionals in case a couple requests assistance.

Certificates

At the completion of any marriage preparation program, certificates should be administered as (1) a way for the couple to verify their participation and completion of the program to their parish priest or minister, (2) a way of acknowledging the effort and investment they made in the program, and (3) a tangible sign to the couple that their engagement is something important to you, the team, and the church. See pages 5 and 6 for examples.

If you do not already have a design for your marriage preparation certificate, you may want to choose one of the following models. We recommend you photocopy them on colored, heavy paper.

Ice-Breakers

We suggest you start a marriage preparation program with some type of warm-up exercise. If your program has several sessions, consider having such an exercise at the beginning of each session if time permits. Some of the exercises listed throughout the couple's edition and leader's edition may be used in such a capacity. Or you may want to use the following exercises.

1. Who's Married to Whom? *(for large group; beginning of program)* Have all the team preparation couples stand up front, men on one side in a row, women on the other side. Have the engaged couples attempt to match up the partners, or have each small group attempt it and then see which small group had the most correct. Make sure that none of the engaged see any of the team members standing with their spouse.

2. Couple to Couple *(small group ice-breaker)* Have two engaged couples interview each other, and then introduce each other to the other couples in the group. Each should find out the following information from the other couple: their names, town(s) of residence, wedding date, honeymoon plans, their favorite pastime as a couple, and the like.

3. Is That Me? *(small group ice-breaker)* Have each person write on a piece of paper their partner's:
- favorite color
- favorite season of the year
- favorite sport or hobby
- favorite song
- eye color
- whether their big toe is longer than the toe next to it

The papers are then handed in to each small group team leader, without names on them and without their partners seeing the answers. The team leader then mixes them up, and reads them out loud one at a time. Each person is then to guess which of the set of answers describes them.

Suggestions for Conducting a Marriage Preparation Program

Most dioceses and churches have well formulated policies and procedures regarding the marriage preparation process within their boundaries. That is why *A Decision to Love* is a flexible workbook, adaptable to most pre-existing programs, and not a prepackaged program in itself. There is no need to re-invent the wheel if you already have a smooth running marriage preparation structure in place. If, however, you are looking for ways to improve your marriage preparation program or if you are in fact just initiating such a program, we offer the following ideas for your consideration.

Basic Marriage Preparation Structure

The basic cycle of most pre-Cana programs consists of a presentation on a given topic by a trained married couple (team couple), followed by an exercise or worksheet for each engaged couple to do and discuss among themselves, followed by a small group exercise. This cycle is repeated, each time focusing on a different topic such as communication, spirituality and religion, finances, and sexuality. This cycle can and should be mixed with various ice-breakers, group exercises, and couple exercises.

Two models for a marriage preparation program using *A Decision to Love* are suggested on pages 8-9.

We encourage you to have the engaged couples sit in small group circles of four or five couples, plus one team couple. This serves three purposes: (1) such an arrangement is better for a more informal and warm atmosphere as opposed to having an auditorium style arrangement; (2) it allows for potentially greater interaction between couples and at least one of the team couples; (3) small group interaction complements the presentations and couple interaction that the engaged are experiencing in your program.

This is to certify that

_____
(bride)

and

_____
(groom)

have completed

A Decision to Love

marriage preparation program.

_____
(coordinator / priest)

_____
(date)

Certification

_____
(bride)

and

_____
(groom)

have completed the

marriage preparation for

_____
(diocese / parish / agency)

_____
(date)

_____
(coordinator / priest)

Use name tags during the program. Couples may complain or joke about this kind of "labeling," but the tags help in developing a sense of connectedness and involvement in the program.

A fitting way to end your marriage preparation program is with some type of prayer service. We offer a sample service later in this workbook.

Presentations

Most marriage preparation programs incorporate presentations by the team couples on the following or similar topics: communication, dealing with disagreements, spirituality and religion, finances, and sexuality. These are the core topics to be covered in any program. You will find outlines for these at the end of Chapters 2, 5, 7, 8. Beyond these, you may want to consider having presentations on the following: family of origin, personality differences, natural family planning, children and parenting, wedding liturgy planning.

Ideally, a presentation is given by one of the team couples, and should last no longer than twenty minutes. The key to a successful talk is for the team couples to be well prepared, relaxed, and genuine. Do not pretend to be something you aren't, or to know something you don't. Be yourself! The talk should reflect your own lived experience as a married couple, struggling and loving through life. You don't have to be a "pro" on the subject you're presenting.

A presenting couple wins over the engaged couples if they state at the beginning of their talk words similar to the following: "We're not professionals. We don't have all the answers. But we are a married couple who cares. We're here to share with you some of our experiences and insights on the subject of...."

One-Day
Marriage Preparation Program
(Model 1)

9:00 AM   Registration. Coffee and donuts

9:30   Welcome. Opening prayer. Introductions of team members

Use of an ice-breaker ("Who's Married to Whom?" for example). Explanation of the purpose of the program. Odds and ends (location of bathrooms, smoking policy, etc.)

10:00   Small group ice-breaker, or blind partner exercise

10:20   Couple exercise: *A Decision to Love*, pages 7-10 (Chapter 1)

10:40   Presentation by team couple: Communication

11:00   Break

11:10   Couple exercise: *A Decision to Love*, pages 15-18 (Chapter 2)

11:30   Small group exercise: *A Decision to Love*, Case Study, page 14 (Chapter 2)

12:10 PM   Lunch

12:45   Couple exercise: *A Decision to Love*. Engaged couple chooses one of the exercises and/or sets of questions from Chapters 3 and 4.

1:15   Presentation by team couple: Sexuality

1:35   Couple exercise: *A Decision to Love*, pages 51-54 (Chapter 5)

1:55   Break

2:00   Small group questions: *A Decision to Love*, page 55 (Chapter 5) and/or small group baby cases, page 63 (Chapter 6)

2:45   Presentation: Finances

3:05   Break, snacks

3:20   Couple pages: *A Decision to Love*, pages 69-73 (Chapter 7)

3:55   Presentation: Spirituality

4:15   Couple pages: *A Decision to Love*, pages 79-82

4:40   Small group exercises: *A Decision to Love*, page 83

5:00   Prayer service

5:30   Dinner (optional)

Three-Evening
Marriage Preparation Program
(Model 2)

First Evening

6:45 PM Registration

7:00 Welcome. Opening prayer. Introductions of team couples.
Explanation of the purpose and procedures of the program. Odds and ends

7:15 Small group ice-breaker

7:30 His and Her Pages: *A Decision to Love*, pages 7-10 (Chapter 1)

7:45 Small group discussion questions: page 11 (Chapter 1)

8:00 Presentation by team couple: Communication

8:20 His and Her Pages: *A Decision to Love*, pages 15-18 (Chapter 2)

8:35 Break

8:40 Small group exercise: *A Decision to Love*, Case Study, page 14
and group section questions: page 19

9:00 Presentation by team couple: Personalities and Separate Pasts

9:15 Couple exercise: *A Decision to Love*, pages 25-32 (Chapter 3)

9:30 Closing remarks

Second Evening

7:00 PM Welcome back. Old business

7:05 Presentation: Family of Origin

7:25 His and Her Pages: *A Decision to Love*, pages 41-44 (Chapter 4)

7:40 Small group exercise: Case study, page 45

7:55 Break

8:00 Presentation: Sexuality

8:20 His and Her Pages, pages 51-54 (Chapter 5)

8:40 Presentation: Children

9:00 His and Her Pages: pages 59-62 (Chapter 6)

9:15 Small group exercise: Baby cases, page 63

9:30 Closing remarks

Third Evening

7:00 PM Welcome back. Old business

7:05 Presentation: Finances

7:25 His and Her Pages: pages 69-72 and Our Section, page 73 (Chapter 7)

7:45 Presentation: Spirituality

8:05 His and Her Pages: pages 79-82 (Chapter 8)

8:25 Break

8:30 Planning the wedding liturgy

8:50 Evaluations and questions

9:00 Prayer service

9:30 Closing remarks

Concluding Prayer Service

REQUIREMENTS Small white taper candles, one per person; large white pillar candle (possibly the church's Paschal Candle) placed up front

Priest/Team Couple Lord Jesus, you have told us that whenever two or more are gathered in your name, that you are there with them. *(Pause)* Lord, we thank you for the gift of love. We thank you for this opportunity to come together, in love, to find out more about ourselves and you. We ask you to strengthen us as a couple, in your love. This we ask through you, our Lord.

All Amen.

Reader An appropriate Scripture reading; for example:
John 17:20–23   Matthew 22:35–40   John 2:1–11
John 15:9–12   1 John 4:7–12   1 Corinthians 12:31—13:8

Priest/Team Couple *(Instructing the engaged couples with words similar to the following)* For our unity candle ceremony, we ask that one person from each small group come up to the Paschal Candle, light his or her candle, and return to the group where the others will light their candle from that one.

Dim the room lights and light the large Paschal Candle. Distribute the small taper candles to each group, one per person.

Priest/Team Couple *(as the Paschal Candle is lit)* Lord Jesus, you are the light of the world. Come into our lives and show us the way.

Pause. Briefly invite the group representative to come forward to light his or her candle and then return to light the candles of the group members.

MUSIC During this part of the ceremony, some appropriate music should be played in the background. A soft instrumental piece works well or a gentle hymn from a Christian musician such as John Michael Talbot, The St. Louis Jesuits, David Haas, Weston Priory.

Priest/Team Couple *(After the song and every candle is lit)* In the midst of the darkness of our daily problems and stresses, God softly comes to us as a light of hope and love. Our God is a God of gentleness, of humor, of invitation, of embracing. May we follow our God and build our relationship on hope, love, gentleness, and humor. *(Pause)*

Come, Lord Jesus, and light our path. For the journey of marriage is long and sometimes dark, but we are filled with hope because you are with us in our life together.

Turn the room lights back on. Briefly instruct the couples to blow out their candles. Keep the Paschal Candle lit.

Priest/Team Couple Now let us join hands and pray in the words that our Savior taught us…

All Our Father, who art in heaven….

Our Decision to Love

Of all the chapters in *A Decision to Love*, this may be the one some team leaders will tend to drop or ignore in their preparation program. Please don't! We find that it is very important for engaged couples to look at the what, why, how, when, and where of their coming together as a couple. The material in this chapter helps the couple to focus on the story of their relationship so far. They are challenged to view their marriage as a mature, Christian *decision* to love.

Whether the engaged man and woman have known each other for ten years or three months, each needs to reflect on their beginning as a couple, which most couples want to do. Because of this, you may want to assign some of the exercises in this chapter as a warm-up at the start of your program.

Depending on the individual maturity of each partner, they may already have a good grasp of the realities of life-long marital love and commitment. Even so, you want to make sure that they are seeing beyond the rose-colored glasses of new love. The Group Section is good in bringing up common cliches and ideas that need to be challenged.

You may want to inform yourself about such things as pre-nuptial agreements, and pre-marital cohabitation. These topics may surface in a small group discussion. As a team, decide beforehand how you want to respond to topics such as these. We recommend that you also find out what the official position of your diocese is on these topics.

Notes

Our Decision to Love

They would have celebrated their second anniversary today. But instead, Sherry finds herself alone. It's hard to figure what went wrong. Somehow, after the wedding everything changed. She discovered so much she hadn't known about Tom. And when it came to the important things, like sharing the chores or having a baby, she realized they hadn't talked about them or agreed upon anything at all. It had felt so wonderful to be in love, who wanted to talk about things that might create hard feelings or cause a fight? She hoped that everything would just kind of work itself out later.

Thinking about it, Sherry remembers the married team couples at her marriage preparation class saying again and again "…engagement is the time to make sure you are ready to marry. It is never too late to wait or to take more time. Be honest with each other. Don't hold anything back. Relationships take work." With a sad smile she remembers how she used to imitate them, to Tom's great amusement, mocking the advice she suspected might be right. Maybe she hadn't been ready. Maybe Tom wasn't her Mr. "Right." But what was she to do after all those years of dating, be alone again? Anyway, the wedding had been planned for months. She wanted to get married.

Now it was clear she had been wrong. If she had known then what she knew now about Tom, herself, and their marriage, she would have taken the advice of those couples and taken a harder look at their relationship before they got married. She would have been more honest, less afraid to talk about what was really bothering her. Maybe Tom would have done

4

NOTE: This page is reproduced from the Couple's Book.

the same. Maybe they could have worked it out. Maybe, maybe, maybe, Sherry thinks. Maybe they could have been celebrating their second anniversary now, together and in love, instead of waiting, each of them alone, for their divorce to be finalized.

Finding Mr. or Ms. "Right" is something we all hope for. Children are raised with "Snow White" or "Cinderella" stereotypes firmly in mind. The Princess-in-distress is rescued by a stunning young Prince who loves her, after which they live happily ever after.

While these images are indeed fairy tale ones, most people unconsciously expect their lives to go in a similar way. When we ask couples in marriage preparation classes what happened when they fell in love, most say it just kind of happened, that it was magical, and that it happened when they weren't quite looking. It was wonderful, a time filled with excitement over plans and the future. These feelings and thoughts about falling in love and about engagement are important to every couple who experiences them. But they need to be balanced with a little reality and some concrete conversations about what your marriage will be like. Excitement and plans don't carry a relationship through the challenges and hard times. Only love with a solid foundation can do that.

Common among engaged couples is an unrealistic expectation we refer to as the myth of marital determinism. It presupposes that the success of your marriage is determined by finding that one right person for you. If you don't happen to find that special partner, then a life of unhappiness and/or divorce is inevitable. But if you do find Mr. or Ms. "Right," a life of joy and peace is sure to follow. One of the many problems with this deterministic view is that when rough times do occur in your marriage, you may be more inclined to view your marital troubles as an indication that you did not find the "right" person. And instead of trying to work together on your relationship, you'll simply agree to break up because "it was a big mistake from the start."

The truth is that there is not just one person in this world for you. There are obviously many people with whom you could be married. But you have chosen this one person. A lifetime of happiness together is not based on chance or on a sort of predetermined cosmic blueprint; rather it is based on the two of you making a mature, Christian decision to love each other...on the day of your wedding, and every day of your married life.

The decision to marry is a decision to love. It's not magic. It's not a roulette game of chance. It's not always easy. Some days

PRE-NUPTIAL AGREEMENTS

A Pre-Nuptial Agreement is a legal contract between two individuals engaged to marry each other, which states in detail how assets will be divided if they divorce in the future. Some see such an agreement as a good insurance policy. But in reality, it may be more of a self-fulfilling predictor of doom. For a couple about to marry in the church, who are about to make a lifelong decision to love in good times and bad, in sickness and in health, for richer or poorer, Pre-Nuptial Agreements may be seen as courting disaster.

The Catholic church has no official teaching regarding such premarital contracts. But, as one priest who works with couples seeking annulments stated, such an agreement at the time of engagement can be construed as a lack of seriousness by the couple toward the permanence of their commitment. There is a sort of "bail out of it if it gets too hot" mentality behind it, and it undermines the need for the engaged couple to seriously consider the commitment they are about to make.

If your partner approaches you with a request to sign such an agreement, especially if it's right before the wedding... Beware! "Honey, I'll love you forever, but please sign on the dotted line."

NOTE: *This page is reproduced from the Couple's Book.*

COHABITATION

"The overall association between premarital cohabitation and subsequent marital stability is striking," states a 1987 study by the National Bureau of Economic Research. More recent studies continue to show that couples who live together before marrying are 50% more likely to divorce than couples who don't cohabit. These findings, substantiated by other independent studies, point to a reality in sharp contrast to commonly-held beliefs of "trial marriages." The fragility of the post-cohabitation marriage was the surprising result of the research for demographers, sociologists, economists, and therapists.

There are many reasons why couples cohabit. Many couples do it for financial reasons, others do it for the convenience. Some couples are engaged to be married, others are attempting to see if they're compatible. Some couples who live together are not sexually active with each other. And others live together as a trial marriage.

A National Council on Family Relations study of over 300 newly-married couples found a higher level of dissatisfaction among those couples who lived a trial marriage before their wedding. Women, in particular, were more unhappy with the quality of communication with their spouses after they married. But why is this the case? And, more importantly, why do couples who live together before marriage have a higher divorce rate?

No one knows for sure. But probably one of the main reasons is that those couples who view premarital cohabitation as a trial marriage are deceiving themselves. As someone once said, living together before marriage in order to prepare for marriage is like taking a bath in order to prepare to swim the English Channel. The best way to prepare for marriage is to talk with each other about every aspect of your relationship, your own personalities, and your future goals. Oddly enough, it seems that premarital cohabitation actually inhibits such basic communication.

the last thing in the world you will want or feel like doing is loving your partner. But those are the days that you say to yourself, "Today, I decide to love my partner." A decision to love demands maturity, selflessness, and a true sense of self-respect.

No couple is 100 percent compatible or perfect for each other. To make your marriage work, you will have to work on it, some days more than others.

This first chapter will focus on your being together and your decision to stay together. Your stories of how you met, and all the details surrounding it, are important because they are the first bricks in the foundation of your relationship and upcoming marriage.

It's important to reflect on the fact that you chose one another and to share with each other the thoughts and feelings associated with it. It is also just as important to look at how those initial feelings and thoughts will affect your future together and your ability to make a lifelong commitment.

In all the chapters of this workbook, we challenge you to challenge yourself and your partner. We encourage you to take this time seriously, to be honest and patient with each other. It is our hope that through these exercises you will discover new things about yourself, your partner, and your relationship which will strengthen your bond and commitment. But since there are some sensitive and often difficult questions, we also realize that there may be times when you will feel shaky and unsure about one or more of these topics. That's O.K. Your engagement is supposed to be the time during which you look at your relationship, discovering those areas that aren't perfect and may require some work. So take your time with this and allow yourselves the opportunity to start your marriage off on the right foot.

NOTE: This page is reproduced from the Couple's Book.

His Page

Answer these questions by yourself and then share your answers with your partner.

1. What did I like about you when we first met?

2. What did I dislike about you?

3. How did I feel about myself when we were first together?

4. What did I first like about us as a couple?

5. What did we decide about living together before marriage and why? How do I feel about our decision?

6. What made us decide to marry? How do I feel about that?

7. Going from being single to being married requires a change in lifestyle. In which of these areas do I think I will need to make changes? In which do I think you will need to make changes?

	ME	YOU	WHY?
Time spent with friends	☐	☐	_____
How money is spent	☐	☐	_____
Hours at work	☐	☐	_____
Leisure time	☐	☐	_____
Time spent with family	☐	☐	_____

7

NOTE: This page is reproduced from the Couple's Book.

8. What have we decided about a pre-nuptial agreement?

   How do I feel about that?

   How will our decision affect our relationship?

9. Who are the people that I feel have helped and supported us as a couple?

   Who do I think have exceptionally good marriages? Why?

10. When I dream about our future, this is what I see in 3 years:

    in 10 years:

NOTE: This page is reproduced from the Couple's Book.

Her Page

Answer these questions by yourself and then share your answers and reflections with your partner.

1. What did I like about you when we first met?

2. What did I dislike about you?

3. How did I feel about myself when we were first together?

4. What did I first like about us as a couple?

5. What did we decide about living together before marriage and why? How do I feel about our decision?

6. What made us decide to marry? How do I feel about that?

7. Going from being single to being married requires a change in lifestyle. In which of these areas do I think I will need to make changes? In which do I think you will need to make changes?

	ME	YOU	WHY?
Time spent with friends	☐	☐	_____
How money is spent	☐	☐	_____
Hours at work	☐	☐	_____
Leisure time	☐	☐	_____
Time spent with family	☐	☐	_____

9

NOTE: This page is reproduced from the Couple's Book.

8. What have we decided about a pre-nuptial agreement?

   How do I feel about that?

   How will our decision affect our relationship?

9. Who are the people that I feel have helped and supported us as a couple?

   Who do I think have exceptionally good marriages? Why?

10. When I dream about our future, this is what I see in 3 years:

    in 10 years:

NOTE: This page is reproduced from the Couple's Book.

Group Section

Answer these questions as a couple and then discuss your answers with other couples in your group.

1. When we hear the phrase "love at first sight" what do we think of? Do I/you agree or disagree with this statement?

2. Do you or I believe that "opposites attract"? Why?

3. What is our definition of "commitment"? How do each of us feel about making a commitment? What are the conditions for making a commitment?

4. What qualities or characteristics have we each seen in other couples who have made a commitment? What are some of the ways a commitment can strengthen or weaken a relationship?

5. How do we feel about pre-nuptial agreements? Do they affect a couple's ability to make and keep a commitment? Why?

Issues of Special Focus

If you have lived together before marrying in the church:

1. We originally decided to live together because…

2. Since we have lived together, how has each of us changed? (Positive/Negative)

3. These are areas which might be beneficial to change…

4. Why do we want to get married now and not just continue to live together?

5. (If you have already been married by a Justice of the Peace or in another church…) Why are we coming to the Catholic church to have our marriage convalidated?

6. What are some of the feelings we have about our upcoming marriage in the church?

7. Will getting married change our relationship? If so, how?

If one or both of you are bringing a child or children into the marriage:

1. How will our marriage affect our child(ren)? How do I think they feel about me? you? Will they feel a part of our new marriage?

2. How do I feel about your child(ren)? How do I feel when I am with them?

3. Have we discussed adopting each other's child(ren)? Do I think that I will feel like a real mom/dad to them? What do we expect from each other as parents?

Please discuss the following questions if they pertain to you.

1. If there is more than eight years difference in our ages, how do I feel about this? How will this affect our relationship?

2. How has it felt to be an interracial couple? How have we dealt with those feelings?

3. How have our ethnic and/or cultural differences affected our relationship?

4. Given some of these differences, how have we been received by each other's families, friends, and communities?

Relationship Check

Each of you should circle the number that best represents how you feel about your relationship after discussing these topics. Remember, you each need to select your own number.

1. very close   2. somewhat close   3. somewhat distant   4. very distant

What do I want to discuss further with you?

NOTE: This page is reproduced from the Couple's Book.

Our Communication/ Negotiation

Good communication practices, and in particular good negotiation skills, are necessary in a good marital relationship. In earlier generations it was just as important, but in some ways it was less difficult and complex than it is today. A couple today is more distracted from home life, less likely to assume the traditional roles in which everyone pretty much knew what was expected. Because they are so busy, they are more likely to spend their time and energy on other people and things than on each other. Therefore, the engaged couples you encounter may need help in focusing their attention and energy on each other, on their relationship.

This chapter offers a variety of ways to help you help the engaged couple. You will find His and Her Pages, Our Section, Group Section, a Case Study, Special Focus Questions, and some Information Boxes. Of particular interest is the "Rules for Disagreements" tear out. You may want to suggest to them that they post it on their refrigerator.

You may also want to consider the following two exercises, called "The Maniac" and "Communication Takes Two," for the presentation on communication and negotiation. The first one is an excellent way to illustrate how perceptions can

differ from one person to another, and thus affect our communication.

"The Maniac"

At the end of the presentation on communication, but before the presenting couple sits down or gives any final words, have one of the other team members jump up and go through a series of fast-paced, disjointed activities in front of everyone. The presenting couple should just step back, stop presenting, act surprised like everyone else, and observe with the rest of the group. "The maniac" could do the following nonsensical activities:

- Jump up and down 3 times
- Run to the light switch and flick the lights off and on 4 times
- Run to one of the seated team members and shout "9, 6, 3, 6, 7"
- Run to an empty chair, sit down, and clap his or her hands 5 times
- Stand up, raise one leg, and shout, "Four score and six years ago..."

And so on.

As a team, figure out the maniac's script ahead

of time. Have fun with it! The more details, actions, and weird statements the maniac makes, the better. The group of engaged couples will obviously be in a state of disbelief, or laughing, depending on how much of a comic the maniac is. But they will catch on to what just happened when the presenting couple tells them what to do next.

They are to write down, in detail, in order of sequence, and with the exact number of times, all the things the maniac did and said. Give them 5 minutes to do this; they are not to talk. Then have them discuss in their small groups their perceptions of what happened, the differences in their perceptions. The key is that everything the maniac did was choreographed, and each team couple has a copy of the script which will help the engaged couples compare the reality of what happened with their perceptions of it.

Point out to the small groups that there was only one reality, but several perceptions and interpretations of what happened. So it is in marital communication: perceptions are often more important than what actually is said or done! We must always confirm what we think we just saw or heard to make sure it's right.

"Communication Takes Two"

For this exercise, you'll need to photocopy the figures on page 23, which are to be distributed to one member of each couple. Be careful that the other member does not see the figures as they are handed out. The purpose of this exercise is to demonstrate that better communication takes place when it's a give and take. One-way communication is ineffective, at best. Two-way communication, although not perfect, makes any task easier.

The person with the photocopy sheet is to describe Figure 1 to his or her partner, who will attempt to draw it. They are to sit back to back. The one who is drawing is not allowed to ask any questions, nor communicate in any way with the partner. After 5 minutes, announce that everyone is to stop Figure 1 and start Figure 2. For this they are allowed to sit facing each other, and the draw-er is allowed to ask questions. Again, allow 5 minutes and then stop the exercise. Then have each couple look over the figures and drawings together and discuss their difficulties of doing Figure 1 and the relative ease of doing Figure 2. This brief exercise is fun and worthwhile. Try it!

Figure One

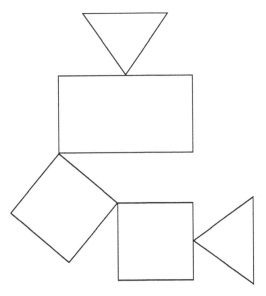

Instructions Put your chairs back to back, so you cannot see each other. You are then to describe how to draw the figure above to your partner without using your hands, and without showing your partner the drawing. No questions are allowed from your partner. Start with the top figure and work your way down.

Figure Two

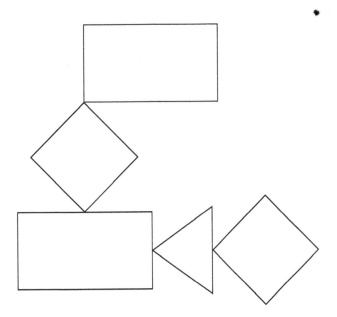

Instructions Turn your chairs around and face each other. You are to describe how to draw the figure above to your partner. You are allowed to use your hands, and your partner is allowed to ask questions.

Our Communication/Negotiation
Talk Outline

1. Introduce self and topic
- Number of years married?
- Any children? Ages?
- Town you live in? Church?
- How long involved as marriage preparation volunteers?
- Any other general information about yourselves?
- What's your topic?
- Why is it important for the engaged couples to hear about this topic?

2. Communication as an art
- Most people assume it just happens naturally.
- Communication is an art requiring practice, energy, attention, skills, patience, and love.
- "Talking is cheap," but true communication is priceless!

3. Communication involves the verbal and the nonverbal
- Talking is verbal communication.
- Active listening, body language, facial expressions, tone of voice, hand gestures, eye contact are all examples of nonverbal communication.
- Nonverbal communication is very important and powerful.
- When there is a conflict between verbals and nonverbals in messages being sent, the receiver will tend to trust the nonverbal message over the verbal message!

4. In a close interpersonal relationship, such as marriage, one of the trickiest types of communication is the "resolution of conflict"—in other words, "fighting"
- Fighting does not have to be *bad*, "*destructive*," or *hurtful*.
- Fighting can be *good*, "*constructive*," and *helpful*.
- Society teaches and provides models for destructive fighting techniques: e.g., yelling, abuse, mind games, silent treatments, name-calling, accusations, threats, etc. All of these are based on the "winner" vs "loser" mentality.
- In your marriage, there should be no winner—no loser. If one of you "wins" an argument, both of you lose.

5. Review the rules for disagreements, "refrigerator copy"

NOTES:
1. Read the couple's and leader's edition chapters on this topic.
2. Lace all talks with personal examples, stories, and real life anecdotes that add color and/or demonstrate what you are talking about.

Notes

CHAPTER TWO

Our Communication/ Negotiation

On his way to work, Carl calls his secretary at the office to remind her to fax certain reports to Chicago. Pam, already at her job, checks her e-mail for any messages regarding the teleconference she will attend later that day. At work, Carl and Pam epitomize modern, sophisticated users of high-tech telecommunications. At home, they are more old-fashioned.

Last night, Carl and Pam had another of their yelling matches on the same old recurring themes: he doesn't listen to her, she nags him. After the argument, he marched off in a silent rage, and she burst into tears. You see, Carl and Pam also epitomize today's young married couple who doesn't know how to communicate.

All around us we notice that in the use of slick telecommunication, today's society is futuristic, light-years ahead of its time. And yet when it comes to interpersonal communication, we often trudge along like grunting cave dwellers.

Communication between a husband and wife is an absolute necessity! But communication involves more than just the mouth and the ears. It involves the total person: eyes, hands, mind…heart. Communication between you and your partner cannot incorporate the cold transmission of information, as it does when Carl is on his cell phone or Pam is at her computer. True communication between loving partners must involve, on both sides, a warm sharing of self. It must involve the total giving of yourself to your partner.

12

NOTE: This page is reproduced from the Couple's Book.

Effective interpersonal communication does not come easily. It requires certain skills that don't come naturally and are therefore often overlooked. These skills need to be learned. Because people in our society are poor at negotiating differences and haven't actually learned any good ways to do it, they often resort to negative behaviors such as yelling, abuse, defensive attitudes, silent treatments, or cheap verbal shots. In the world outside your marriage, these techniques will classify you as aggressive at worst. In the world of your marriage, they may destroy the relationship. Destructive fighting tears down, destroys, takes life away. Constructive fighting builds up, enhances, gives life to the marriage.

We have two little boys. And we're constantly amazed at how many bumps, bruises, and scrapes they get. But we're even more amazed at how fast the "boo-boos" heal. Their young bodies quickly recuperate. Though we're not ancient, we notice that on our bodies such scrapes and bumps take a lot longer to heal. And individuals in the twilight years of their lives realize that some bruises never heal.

Your marriage is similar. While it's still very young, it has an amazing capacity for self-mending. The two of you are able to bounce back from a destructive fight relatively quickly, and the fight leaves no apparent scar. But as your marriage matures, its resilience diminishes. Scars form. Repercussions from destructive fights remain.

This is why it is very important to establish good skills for fair fighting now while your marriage is young. Disagreements are inevitable, even necessary for a strong, lasting relationship. But they can be expressed in a life-giving and constructive way. If you are practicing destructive fighting techniques now, chances are you will begin to develop more lasting scars.

In this chapter we will focus on how well you think you communicate as a couple. The questions will reflect this focus, and will also ask you to look at how you fight. We have also listed

FIGHT!

Often people assume fighting is bad. Actually, for an intimate, exclusive relationship such as marriage, fighting not only has the potential to be good, but is also necessary. But in order for the fighting to be good for the relationship, it must be constructive and not destructive.

A constructive fight is a "fair" fight in which both sides win. A good way to determine the quality of your fighting is to ask yourself: "How do I feel about myself after we fight?" It's not a question of whether you got your way or "won" the fight. Rather, it's a question of whether the process you both used to negotiate your differences is "life-enhancing" to you and your relationship. If you feel put-down, guilty, revengeful, manipulated or manipulative, hateful, or smug after you've fought, then chances are your fighting is taking a destructive toll on your relationship.

Constructive fighting should build up, enhance, fortify, and actually nurture your relationship, regardless of who "wins." The following is a good process for dealing with your differences that may enable your fighting to be life-enhancing and not life-taking from your relationship.

The next time you have a disagreement, sit down and face each other. Using the Rules for Disagreements in this chapter, take turns stating your side of the issue. However, before voicing your views, you must restate the ideas and feelings expressed by your partner and do so to the satisfaction of your partner. This is difficult to do. The assumption here is that if I can tell you what you said and felt, then I truly heard and understood you. If I can't, then either I was not fully present to you while you spoke, or else you were not sufficiently clear. This process of fighting motivates each of you to clarify your thoughts before you speak and to concentrate on what your partner is truly saying and not on what your response is going to be.

"LISTEN"

The Chinese written word for "listen," *ting*, is a composite of four other words: *er - dr* (ear), *tu -lau* (mind), *yen - jin* (eye), and *shem* (heart). The combination of these four vital parts leads to effective listening. We must not only hear with our ears, we must also listen with our minds, our eyes, and our hearts.

13

NOTE: This page is reproduced from the Couple's Book.

FUNNY AS A KNIFE!

"Oh, come on! I was only kidding. Can't you take a joke?"

Have you ever heard or spoken words similar to these to your partner?

Humor is one thing. But intentional belittlement of your partner, especially in front of others, is not only unfair but also abusive. A lot of harm is done in relationships when one partner degrades the other in public under the guise of humor. Men especially will often try to prove how witty they are, as a type of machismo, by making disparaging remarks about their mate in a comical fashion. Nervous laughter often is the response from the partner and those around.

But let's be clear, there's more than just a good time going on. Such grandstanding is actually very immature and irresponsible behavior that may cut your partner's spirit like a knife. No one wants to be the butt of jokes, especially when it's coming from the one you love! If you feel your partner verbally abuses you in front of your friends under the facade of joking, talk to him/her about it. State how it makes you feel. And if you are in the practice of having a good laugh at the expense of your partner… Stop! You're probably not as funny or witty as you may think, and you're definitely hurting your partner's feelings.

some tried and true rules for disagreements; you can tear this page out and hang it on your refrigerator.

One final note. We have found that one of the best ways to witness your partner's true colors before you marry is to have a fight of substantial weight. We don't mean a little nagging, recurring squabble, but a serious disagreement. Too often engaged couples avoid discussing an issue they know will erupt into a fight, hoping that somehow the wedding will make it all O.K. We think that this is a mistake. We're not advocating that you fabricate a fight just because we suggest it will help your relationship! Rather we are saying that you should not avoid fighting before the wedding (or after the wedding). When you're angry, upset, or hurt, and you attempt to communicate that to the one you love, your true self emerges. Facades tumble. Pretenses vanish. How you "look" is no longer important. You're hurt or angry and you want your partner to know it! If you don't like what you see in your partner or yourself when you fight, then you probably won't like what you see in your marriage down the road. The quality of your fighting now, before you marry, may indicate the quality of your future marriage.

CASE STUDY

BILL AND CHRISSY

"I'm furious at you! You made me feel foolish at the pizzeria! Why did you do that?" Chrissy demands. Bill, with a little grin on his face, calmly responds. "Listen, I was only joking. Everyone knew I wasn't serious when I said that you talked so much that my ears hurt. Besides, everyone laughed. You always blow things out of proportion!"

"You jerk!" she explodes. "You think you're so smug. How would you like it if the next time we're with our friends I 'joke' about your problems with your mom?"

"You'd better not!" Bill says sternly. "Besides, I don't think you fully understand that situation yourself!" He storms off to the car and drives away.

? *What makes this fight such a destructive one? Why does each of them say and do things that are unfair and hurt the other?*

NOTE: This page is reproduced from the Couple's Book.

His Page

Answer these questions by yourself and then share your answers with your partner.

1. I think that I communicate with you: ☐ very well   ☐ well   ☐ poorly   ☐ not as well as I could

    How does my answer make me feel?

2. I think that you communicate with me: ☐ very well   ☐ well   ☐ poorly   ☐ not as well as I could

    How does my answer make me feel?

3. What was the last big decision we made together?

    Who made the decision?

4. How did we come to the decision?

5. Am I happy with how decisions are made in our relationship, or are there things I would like to see changed? Explain.

6. If we couldn't come to a decision that both of us agreed upon, what would we do?

    ☐ I would decide.   ☐ We would compromise on an alternative.

    ☐ You would decide.   ☐ We would forget about the whole thing.

    ☐ We would ask someone.   ☐ Other _____

7. I can always tell when you are angry because...

15

NOTE: This page is reproduced from the Couple's Book.

8. When we have a big fight, what do we each do?

ME	YOU		ME	YOU		ME	YOU	
☐	☐	yell	☐	☐	become sarcastic	☐	☐	don't listen
☐	☐	become silent	☐	☐	make a joke out of it	☐	☐	hit my partner
☐	☐	cry	☐	☐	say insulting things	☐	☐	listen
☐	☐	talk about how I feel	☐	☐	bring up past issues	☐	☐	walk off
☐	☐	throw or hit things						

9. What was our last argument about?

   Do I think that you understood my side?

   Do I think that I understood your side?

10. Whenever we fight, I feel...

11. The topics that usually start a fight between us are:

   a.

   b.

12. When I am angry with you, I...

13. When you are sad or hurt or upset by a fight, I feel...

14. Do I ever fear that you will become violent and hurt me or my child(ren)? Explain.

15. Communication in my family of origin meant...

16

NOTE: This page is reproduced from the Couple's Book.

Her Page

Answer these questions by yourself and then share your answers with your partner.

1. I think that I communicate with you: ☐ very well ☐ well ☐ poorly ☐ not as well as I could

   How does my answer make me feel?

2. I think that you communicate with me: ☐ very well ☐ well ☐ poorly ☐ not as well as I could

   How does my answer make me feel?

3. What was the last big decision we made together?

   Who made the decision?

4. How did we come to the decision?

5. Am I happy with how decisions are made in our relationship, or are there things I would like to see changed? Explain.

6. If we couldn't come to a decision that both of us agreed upon, what would we do?

   ☐ I would decide.   ☐ We would compromise on an alternative.

   ☐ You would decide.   ☐ We would forget about the whole thing.

   ☐ We would ask someone.   ☐ Other _____

7. I can always tell when you are angry because…

17

NOTE: This page is reproduced from the Couple's Book.

8. When we have a big fight, what do we each do?

ME YOU

- ☐ ☐ yell
- ☐ ☐ become silent
- ☐ ☐ cry
- ☐ ☐ talk about how I feel
- ☐ ☐ throw or hit things

ME YOU

- ☐ ☐ become sarcastic
- ☐ ☐ make a joke out of it
- ☐ ☐ say insulting things
- ☐ ☐ bring up past issues

ME YOU

- ☐ ☐ don't listen
- ☐ ☐ hit my partner
- ☐ ☐ listen
- ☐ ☐ walk off

9. What was our last argument about?

Do I think that you understood my side?

Do I think that I understood your side?

10. Whenever we fight, I feel...

11. The topics that usually start a fight between us are:

a.

b.

12. When I am angry with you, I...

13. When you are sad or hurt or upset by a fight, I feel...

14. Do I ever fear that you will become violent and hurt me or my child(ren)? Explain.

15. Communication in my family of origin meant...

NOTE: This page is reproduced from the Couple's Book.

Group Section

Discuss these questions with a group of other engaged couples.

1. What are some "mind games" couples play when they're fighting? (Eg., trying to make your partner feel guilty, waiting for your partner to ask you if there is something wrong, or denying that there is a problem to be talked about.)
2. What do you think is meant by this statement: A couple needs to communicate not only with their ears and mouth, but also with their hearts, their heads, and their souls?
3. In many homes people communicate through sarcasm, teasing, and violence. How can you avoid these behaviors? Discuss why they are destructive.

Our Section

Discuss and answer these questions together as a couple.

1. What couple do we know who we both think demonstrates good communication skills? (You must agree here. If you can't agree on a couple, discuss why not.)
2. In what ways could we communicate better? What changes are each of us willing to make?
3. In looking at how we communicate, is there anything that I/you would like to change? Are there areas where I/you think we need to learn more skills?
4. What do we each need from the other in order to feel listened to and understood?
5. How can we encourage and respect each other's thoughts, feelings, and/or decisions even when we don't agree with what the other is saying/doing?
6. How was the communication in my/your family when we were growing up? How has this affected us in the way each of us communicates with others? with each other?

Issues of Special Focus

If one or both of you are bringing a child(ren) to this marriage:

1. How do I feel about the communication with my child(ren)? with your child(ren)? Is there anything that I would want to change?
2. How will you as a couple deal with a conflict when it occurs between the parent and the child(ren)? The new partner and the child(ren)?
3. If I ever found myself physically abusing your child, I would _____.
4. How will you maintain a working relationship with the parent that the child(ren) do not live with if the child(ren) have contact with him/her?
5. How were anger and/or disagreements handled in my/your previous marriage? What would I like to do differently this time?

Relationship Check

Each of you should circle the number that best represents how you feel about your relationship after discussing these topics. Remember, you each need to select your own number.

1. very close   2. somewhat close   3. somewhat distant   4. very distant

What do I want to discuss further with you?

NOTE: This page is reproduced from the Couple's Book.

RULES FOR DISAGREEMENTS

1 **Use "I" Statements and Avoid "You" Statements**
I put you on the defensive if I start my sentence with "You…"

2 **Use "Heart" Statements and Avoid "Head" Statements**
I will tell you how I feel (not what I think). Please understand that my feelings are mine, that I have a right to them…and don't judge them.

3 **Don't Interrupt**
In this way, I will not only "hear" you, but I will truly "listen" to you and try to understand your view without rushing in with my own views. Then, please listen to me without interrupting.

4 **Don't "De-personalize" the Fight**
I will maintain eye contact with you. I will stop whatever else I am doing (like watching TV). I will not call you names, or trivialize your view by making a "joke" out of it. I will sit down with you and talk it through. I won't walk out, unless we both agree to cool down for a while. Please treat me with the same respect.

5 **Fight Lovingly**
I understand that "fighting" and "loving" are not necessarily different. Even in my anger and rage, I love you. I promise that even in the midst of our fighting, I will not say or do anything that will belittle or destroy you or our relationship. Please deal with me and our relationship in the same nurturing way.

6 **Keep It Simple**
I will try as hard as possible to be clear and stick to the issue at hand. Because I may be emotional, angry, or hurting, it may be difficult for me to talk. But I promise to try. If nothing else, I will tell you, "I feel angry" or "I feel hurt." I ask you to also be clear and to not bring up past issues.

7 **Don't Play Mind Games**
I will always try to be direct and sincere with you; I will not play games or fool with the "trust" and "honesty" that our relationship is built on. I ask that you try to be direct with me too, avoiding any mental or emotional games.

8 **Don't Abuse**
I realize that I know things about you that no one else knows. I know what topics are sensitive to you. I know your weak spots. I promise not to abuse this almost-sacred knowledge I have. I promise not to abuse you. I ask that you not abuse me, for I too am vulnerable to you.

9 **Don't Be Afraid to Seek Professional Help**
If our fighting happens more often and increases in its intensity and we feel that our differences are becoming unmanageable, then let's contact a counselor. I realize that we may feel foolish, embarrassed, or unsure as we seek this help. But I also realize it's better to err on the side of caution than to watch our marriage die.

NOTE: This page is reproduced from the Couple's Book.

Our Separate Pasts and Personalities

How many times have you heard a married person (or yourself) observe, "It's the little things in marriage that build up to be big things....and big problems"? Whether it's the socks left in the middle of the floor, the toothpaste tube squeezed in the middle, the forgotten anniversary, or the amount of television watched, the "little" annoyances in any close relationship can lead to fights, anger, and negative feelings if not dealt with in a healthy way.

This chapter helps the engaged couple examine how they are different. They realize that not only are they different, but that their differences are often based on the fact that they are two different personalities with two different histories.

The Personality Assessment is an enjoyable and enlightening exercise. Typically when the couples are comparing their answers you'll hear some laughter and joking, which is good. But you may also hear and see some serious discussions going on. Couples are sometimes amazed by how they see each other and themselves. After the Personality Assessment, you may want to present the case study of Kevin and Emily for a small group discussion.

The Alcoholism Questionnaire is something you may want to recommend they complete on their own time, at home. Point out the Resource Appendix in the back of their book. And have on hand the local numbers for Alcoholics Anonymous (A.A.), Narcotics Anonymous (N.A.), and Al-Anon.

> "Familiarity breeds contempt." AESOP
>
> "Familiarity breeds contempt—and children." MARK TWAIN
>
> "Though familiarity may not breed contempt, it takes the edge off admiration." WILLIAM HAZLITT

KEVIN AND EMILY

In the Personality Assessment, Kevin rated himself, in order, as Mother Teresa, St. Francis, Teddy Roosevelt, Leonardo Da Vinci, and Mickey Mouse. Emily rated Kevin in order as the Statue of Liberty, Peter Pan, Archie Bunker, Evel Knievel, and Leonardo Da Vinci. Assuming that neither Kevin nor Emily are 100 percent correct in their assessments of Kevin, what do they need to talk over about their personality reviews of Kevin? How does Kevin see himself? How does Emily see Kevin? What is the overall picture that they each paint of Kevin? How are they different? How are they the same?

Notes

CHAPTER THREE

Our Separate Pasts and Personalities

"Flannel shirts! I love flannel shirts. I'm a flannel shirt type of guy. Well, she doesn't like flannel shirts! She wants me to walk around the house in dress shirts all day. In fact, she threw out all my flannel shirts!" Stephen was becoming increasingly upset as he relived story upon story of how Megan, his wife of only one year, was attempting to change him. "The other day, we got into a big fight after a party," he continued. "Miss 'Life of the Party' over there was angry at me because I wanted to come home early. Heck, I was tired!"

"Well, if you weren't such a bump-on-a-log, if you could just loosen up once in a while," she shouted back, "then maybe you'd have some fun too!"

Megan was trying to change not only how he dressed, but how he spoke, how he carried himself in public, how he planned things, even how he thought. She was trying to mold him into something he was not. She was doomed to fail, of course. But, unfortunately, she didn't realize that she was also dooming his trust in her.

And Stephen, likewise, was attempting to subdue Megan's spirited personality.

Often the very characteristics that first attracted us to our partners are the very characteristics we eventually attempt to change. Opposites may attract...but familiarity also breeds contempt. And this often leads to attempts at making your partner more like you.

When they first started dating, Megan and Stephen's opposite personalities balanced each other well. Megan found Stephen's quiet, introverted

21

NOTE: This page is reproduced from the Couple's Book.

REMARRIAGE

The number of remarriages in the U.S. has increased dramatically since the 1970s. There are more than 1 million remarriages a year in this country. And many of these are not only second marriages for one or both partners, but third or fourth. About one-third of all Americans will eventually remarry at least once in their lives.

Naturally those who have divorced hope that the new marriage will be a better union than the others were. Unfortunately, the divorce rate for remarriage is higher than for first marriages. Sixty percent of re-marriages end in divorce.

People who marry again face stresses and challenges that often are ignored or underestimated until it is too late. Dealing with former spouses, stepchildren, financial problems, relocation, and low self-esteem stemming from the divorce are the major sources of stress. But of all these, most experts agree that the one element which causes the most instability in remarriages is the presence of stepchildren. About 40 percent of remarriages involve stepchildren. And the relationship between them and the stepparent may cause significant problems in the marriage.

ways a source of comfort and rest from her hectic pace as an emergency room nurse. And he was attracted to Megan's energetic and outgoing approach to life. However, after a year of marriage, Megan wished Stephen wanted to go out more with their friends, and Stephen wished Megan would slow down and cool it once in awhile.

We're happy to report that five years later, after some marriage counseling and a lot of hard work, Megan and Stephen are happily married. When they look back over their years of turmoil, they agree that the biggest lesson they learned is that you cannot change another person. People change only if they want to.

This chapter will focus on your different personalities. "Oh, but we're so much alike," you may say. Well, unless you're marrying a clone of yourself, the two of you are different. No two people are completely compatible. To one degree or another, you and your partner are incompatible. And many of your differences are based on the simple fact that you, as individuals, have different personalities. Not to acknowledge your partner's unique personality is to deny your partner the respect he or she deserves.

What do we mean when we say that you have different personalities? Quickly, answer these questions to yourself: Which one of you is more outgoing and social? Which one is more

CO-DEPENDENCY

An alcoholic has an uncontrollable dependency on alcohol; a drug addict has a dependency on drugs; a compulsive gambler depends on gambling. A co-dependent is someone who has a "dependency" on someone else, usually a loved one who is an alcoholic or addict of some type. The common link between all of these dependencies, whether on a substance, a behavior, or a person, is the unhealthy obsessive/compulsive behavior that consumes the dependent individual.

Alcoholism and addictions affect not only the alcoholic or addict, but everyone close to this person. Co-dependency refers to the maladaptive behavior, the irrational thinking, and the suppressed but intense feelings that take place as a result of the addiction of a loved one. Co-dependents stop living for themselves. Co-dependents become more and more enmeshed in the bizarre world of the addict. Co-dependents may even take the responsibility for the alcoholic's drinking, and may believe that if they only did "this" or "that," the person would stop drinking.

Co-dependents may believe they can cure or control the addiction but may subconsciously facilitate it by denying the problem and helping to hide it from neighbors, parents, or the boss.

Co-dependents are not happy people. Their obsession with the alcoholic's drinking or the addict's unhealthy behavior overrides all other thoughts, feelings, plans, goals, all enjoyment in life. A co-dependent, like the addicted person, leads a dysfunctional life. And after a while, the co-dependent suppresses all personal needs and feelings. We have stressed elsewhere and will emphasize here, if you find yourself in such an unhealthy situation, seek professional counseling. It may be one of the most loving and healthy things you can do for yourself, your partner, and your relationship.

22

NOTE: This page is reproduced from the Couple's Book.

organized? More emotional? More stubborn? More confident? More idealistic? More romantic? More financially minded? You see, you are different. And it's surprising how the "little" differences between you now can grow into "big" differences down the road.

While dating, he may find it cute how she absentmindedly misplaces her keys. Or she may find him attractive when he aggressively takes control of a situation. But after a year or two of marriage, of constantly misplaced items and aggressive behavior, the cuteness and attractiveness of their differences may become problematic. And each may attempt to change the other.

In their book *Please Understand Me*, David Keirsey and Marilyn Bates contend that the primary source of fractured marriages is a phenomenon they call "The Pygmalion Project." This refers to the attempts of some spouses to transform their partners into copies of themselves. They write: "It is as if the marriage license is construed as a sculptor's license, giving each spouse the warrant to chisel away until the other becomes the spit and image of the sculptor."

You cannot change your partner. Look at him or her long and hard...because what you see now is basically what you'll have ten, fifteen, forty years from now. Your partner will obviously change a little, but his or her basic personality will remain the same. And if your partner does change, it will have to be your partner's decision, not yours.

Included in this chapter is a short his and her personality assessment that will introduce you to your own personality traits and those of your partner. It has been designed to be an enjoyable, non-threatening way for you to think about and discuss your differences and similarities. The events of our pasts are an important part of who we are and can therefore have an effect on our relationships. Like personalities, they too are something that cannot be altered. When left undiscussed, the events of our past have potential to become a source of conflict.

Old boyfriends, girlfriends, spouses, and families of origin are permanent chapters in your book of life. For that reason, this chapter will also focus you and your partner on your individual pasts and invite you to share more about them with each other. We believe that by sharing about your past before you are married, you are saving your partner and your relationship from any surprises or old patterns of behavior that will eventually surface. Honesty is a crucial component for a successful marriage.

SPOUSE ABUSE

Spousal abuse, especially wife abuse, is considered to be the most common unreported crime in the U.S. Approximately twenty million women are repeatedly abused by men whom they know. Worse, only about 10 percent of all abuse cases are reported to authorities.

What is spouse abuse or battering? It's the repeated subjecting of one person to any forceful physical or psychological behavior by another without any regard for her or his rights. Battering doesn't develop overnight. There are usually early indicators of potential wife or husband abuse.

1. Does your partner ever go into a rage of unreasonable anger?

2. Is your partner physically violent?

3. Does your partner have a poor self-image?

4. Do you feel that it is your fault if your partner hits you or verbally abuses you?

5. Does your partner abuse alcohol or drugs?

6. Were you or your partner physically or sexually abused as a child?

7. Does your partner consistently blame you for his/her problems?

8. Do you find yourself rationalizing or justifying your partner's anger or violence?

If your answer is "yes" to any of these questions, seek professional counseling before you marry. If physical abuse is already present in your relationship, then call off the wedding now! Things will not get better. They will get worse! For further guidance, contact a counseling agency or a local advocacy group for battered spouses.

23

NOTE: This page is reproduced from the Couple's Book.

Finally, if abuse (drug or alcohol, physical or emotional), addictions (gambling, overeating, drugs, alcohol, sex, spending), mental illness, or other unusual behaviors have been a part of your life or your family's past or present, talk to your partner about it now. Seek help if you find your behavior is beyond your control. And if your partner has a problem, encourage him or her to seek help too. Problems such as these don't go away. They only get worse. Don't delude yourself with thinking that your love or this marriage will make it all O.K. While love and marriage might serve as temporary distractions, problematic behavior will drag you along with it and destroy your marriage in the process.

ALCOHOLISM/SUBSTANCE ABUSE

1. Addiction to alcohol and drugs (illegal and prescription) is much more common and widespread than most of us realize.

2. Alcoholism is a disease! It's not the result of weak will power, poor moral character, or some deficient personality.

3. Alcoholism does not discriminate….anyone can have the disease: females and males, whites and blacks, poor and rich, young and old!

4. There is no cure for alcoholism or any addictions. If you are an addict, you will always be an addict. Total abstinence from alcohol and drugs for alcoholics and drug abusers is the only way to stop the effects of these addictive behaviors.

5. Addictions are extremely powerful! Denial of the problem by the addicted person and loved ones is the common way of dealing with such an overwhelming problem.

6. Self-acceptance is the first step toward recovery. Active and ongoing participation in support groups is crucial to the addict's recovery.

7. Addictions not only affect the addict, but also the addict's loved ones, both family and friends. They too need to seek support and help from groups such as Al-Anon and Ala-Teen.

8. Alcoholism is a progressive disease and, like all addictions, leads ultimately to death.

9. An active addict will stop at nothing to continue the addictive behavior.

10. Often family members will subconsciously adapt their behavior, thinking, and feelings to accommodate the addicted person's bizarre behavior. This is known as co-dependence. People who are co-dependent need to seek help for themselves.

24

NOTE: This page is reproduced from the Couple's Book.

His Personality Assessment

From the following list, pick five or more "characters" that you feel reflect your personality the best. Rank them in order from 1–5, with 1 being the most like you. Then do the same for your partner. Don't let the gender of the character determine your selections. Rather, let the images they suggest guide you.

ME YOU

☐ ☐ **Peter Pan** *perpetual child*

☐ ☐ **Gumby** *flexible*

☐ ☐ **Statue of Liberty** *"Let me show the way"*

☐ ☐ **Bambi** *meek and gentle*

☐ ☐ **General Patton** *takes control*

☐ ☐ **Oscar the Grouch** *pessimist, sour*

☐ ☐ **Mother Teresa** *saves the world*

☐ ☐ **Albert Einstein** *scientist*

☐ ☐ **St. Francis** *back to nature*

☐ ☐ **Don Juan** *romantic*

☐ ☐ **Boy Scout** *trustworthy*

☐ ☐ **George Washington** *"never tell a lie"*

☐ ☐ **Charlie Brown** *loner*

☐ ☐ **Rambo** *"take no prisoners"*

☐ ☐ **Snoopy** *party animal*

☐ ☐ **Evel Knievel** *thrill seeker*

☐ ☐ **Teddy Bear** *soft and cuddly*

ME YOU

☐ ☐ **Warren Buffett** *all business*

☐ ☐ **Teddy Roosevelt**
       "talk softly and carry a big stick"

☐ ☐ **Mickey Mouse** *"Fun! fun! fun!"*

☐ ☐ **Archie Bunker** *opinionated*

☐ ☐ **Rhett Butler** *"I don't give a damn"*

☐ ☐ **Dear Abby** *problem solver*

☐ ☐ **Fred Flintstone** *loud*

☐ ☐ **Frank Lloyd Wright** *the architect*

☐ ☐ **Sandra Day O'Connor** *the judge*

☐ ☐ **Leonardo da Vinci** *artist*

☐ ☐ **Miss Manners**
       "a proper way for everything"

☐ ☐ **Henry Kissinger** *negotiator*

☐ ☐ **George Burns** *the comic*

☐ ☐ **Bozo** *the clown*

☐ ☐ **Robert Frost** *the poet*

Discuss Your "Characters"

Now compare the characters that you have selected for yourself and for your partner and discuss them. Use these to get your discussion started:

1. Discuss each character and why you or your partner selected it.

2. Do you feel that your partner's selections correspond with the way you see yourself? Why?

3. Do these characters paint an overall picture of each of you?

4. Do any of these characters point out behaviors that you or your partner might want to change?

25

NOTE: This page is reproduced from the Couple's Book.

His Drinking Questionnaire

This test, used by Johns Hopkins University Hospital in Baltimore, is helpful in determining whether someone has a drinking problem.

Answer these questions (yes "y" or no "n") for yourself and your partner as best you can. Compare your answers with your partner's. Each question may also be used to determine drug addiction by replacing "drinking" with "doing drugs."

ME YOU

☐ ☐ Do you lose time from work due to drinking?

☐ ☐ Is drinking making your home life unhappy?

☐ ☐ Do you drink because you are shy with other people?

☐ ☐ Is drinking affecting your reputation?

☐ ☐ Have you ever felt remorse after drinking?

☐ ☐ Have you gotten into financial difficulties as a result of drinking?

☐ ☐ Do you turn to lower companions and an inferior environment when drinking?

☐ ☐ Does your drinking make you careless of your family's welfare?

☐ ☐ Has your ambition decreased since drinking?

☐ ☐ Do you crave a drink at a definite time daily?

☐ ☐ Do you want a drink the next morning?

☐ ☐ Does drinking cause you to have difficulty in sleeping?

☐ ☐ Has your efficiency decreased since drinking?

☐ ☐ Is drinking jeopardizing your job or business?

☐ ☐ Do you drink to escape from worries or trouble?

☐ ☐ Do you drink alone?

☐ ☐ Have you ever had a complete loss of memory as a result of drinking?

☐ ☐ Has your physician ever treated you for drinking?

☐ ☐ Do you drink to build up your self-confidence?

☐ ☐ Have you ever been to a hospital or institution on account of drinking?

If you have answered YES to some of these questions, this is an indication that you may have a drinking problem. You and your partner need to talk about this.

Unfortunately, the abuse of alcohol, drugs, sex, food, gambling, and spending is becoming increasingly more common in today's world. The effects of this abuse are devastating to the individual caught in the negative behavior and to those people who love the abuser.

As an engaged couple, you should look seriously and honestly at any area in your lives that might point out behavior that is out of control. The following behaviors may indicate serious problems: frequent drunkenness from alcohol or highs from drugs; promiscuity; use of pornography or inappropriate sexual behavior; food binges or crash diets; spending large amounts of money on races, slot machines, or lotteries; and sky high credit card usage or shopping binges.

If any of these fits either you or your partner, stop and talk about it. Get help! Don't try to pretend that the problem is not there. Be honest with yourself and your partner and get help in order to get your life back under control. Marriage will not change these behaviors.

26

NOTE: This page is reproduced from the Couple's Book.

Her Personality Assessment

From the following list, pick five or more "characters" that you feel reflect your personality the best. Rank them in order from 1–5, with 1 being the most like you. Then do the same for your partner. Don't let the gender of the character determine your selections. Rather, let the images they suggest guide you.

ME YOU

☐ ☐ **Peter Pan** *perpetual child*
☐ ☐ **Gumby** *flexible*
☐ ☐ **Statue of Liberty** *"Let me show the way"*
☐ ☐ **Bambi** *meek and gentle*
☐ ☐ **General Patton** *takes control*
☐ ☐ **Oscar the Grouch** *pessimist, sour*
☐ ☐ **Mother Teresa** *saves the world*
☐ ☐ **Albert Einstein** *scientist*
☐ ☐ **St. Francis** *back to nature*
☐ ☐ **Don Juan** *romantic*
☐ ☐ **Boy Scout** *trustworthy*
☐ ☐ **George Washington** *"never tell a lie"*
☐ ☐ **Charlie Brown** *loner*
☐ ☐ **Rambo** *"take no prisoners"*
☐ ☐ **Snoopy** *party animal*
☐ ☐ **Evel Knievel** *thrill seeker*
☐ ☐ **Teddy Bear** *soft and cuddly*

ME YOU

☐ ☐ **Warren Buffett** *all business*
☐ ☐ **Teddy Roosevelt** *"talk softly and carry a big stick"*
☐ ☐ **Mickey Mouse** *"Fun! fun! fun!"*
☐ ☐ **Archie Bunker** *opinionated*
☐ ☐ **Rhett Butler** *"I don't give a damn"*
☐ ☐ **Dear Abby** *problem solver*
☐ ☐ **Fred Flintstone** *loud*
☐ ☐ **Frank Lloyd Wright** *the architect*
☐ ☐ **Sandra Day O'Connor** *the judge*
☐ ☐ **Leonardo da Vinci** *artist*
☐ ☐ **Miss Manners** *"a proper way for everything"*
☐ ☐ **Henry Kissinger** *negotiator*
☐ ☐ **George Burns** *the comic*
☐ ☐ **Bozo** *the clown*
☐ ☐ **Robert Frost** *the poet*

Discuss Your "Characters"

Now compare the characters that you have selected for yourself and for your partner and discuss them. Use these to get your discussion started:

1. Discuss each character and why you or your partner selected it.

2. Do you feel that your partner's selections correspond with the way you see yourself? Why?

3. Do these characters paint an overall picture of each of you?

4. Do any of these characters point out behaviors that you or your partner might want to change?

27

NOTE: This page is reproduced from the Couple's Book.

Her Drinking Questionnaire

This test, used by Johns Hopkins University Hospital in Baltimore, is helpful in determining whether someone has a drinking problem.

Answer these questions (yes "y" or no "n") for yourself and your partner as best you can. Compare your answers with your partner's. Each question may also be used to determine drug addiction by replacing "drinking" with "doing drugs."

ME YOU

☐ ☐ Do you lose time from work due to drinking?
☐ ☐ Is drinking making your home life unhappy?
☐ ☐ Do you drink because you are shy with other people?
☐ ☐ Is drinking affecting your reputation?
☐ ☐ Have you ever felt remorse after drinking?
☐ ☐ Have you gotten into financial difficulties as a result of drinking?
☐ ☐ Do you turn to lower companions and an inferior environment when drinking?
☐ ☐ Does your drinking make you careless of your family's welfare?
☐ ☐ Has your ambition decreased since drinking?
☐ ☐ Do you crave a drink at a definite time daily?
☐ ☐ Do you want a drink the next morning?
☐ ☐ Does drinking cause you to have difficulty in sleeping?
☐ ☐ Has your efficiency decreased since drinking?
☐ ☐ Is drinking jeopardizing your job or business?
☐ ☐ Do you drink to escape from worries or trouble?
☐ ☐ Do you drink alone?
☐ ☐ Have you ever had a complete loss of memory as a result of drinking?
☐ ☐ Has your physician ever treated you for drinking?
☐ ☐ Do you drink to build up your self-confidence?
☐ ☐ Have you ever been to a hospital or institution on account of drinking?

If you have answered YES to some of these questions, this is an indication that you may have a drinking problem. You and your partner need to talk about this.

Unfortunately, the abuse of alcohol, drugs, sex, food, gambling, and spending is becoming increasingly more common in today's world. The effects of this abuse are devastating to the individual caught in the negative behavior and to those people who love the abuser.

As an engaged couple, you should look seriously and honestly at any area in your lives that might point out behavior that is out of control. The following behaviors may indicate serious problems: frequent drunkenness from alcohol or highs from drugs; promiscuity; use of pornography or inappropriate sexual behavior; food binges or crash diets; spending large amounts of money on races, slot machines, or lotteries; and sky high credit card usage or shopping binges.

If any of these fits either you or your partner, stop and talk about it. Get help! Don't try to pretend that the problem is not there. Be honest with yourself and your partner and get help in order to get your life back under control. Marriage will not change these behaviors.

28

NOTE: This page is reproduced from the Couple's Book.

His Page

Answer these questions by yourself. When you are finished discuss your answers and reflections with your partner.

1. Do I feel that you are trying to change me? How?

2. How do I think that our personalities complement each other?

3. How do I feel about discussing my past relationships? Can I be honest? Do I think that you really listen to me and understand?

4. How do I feel about discussing your past relationships?

5. Am I concerned about my use of drugs or alcohol? spending habits? sexual activity? eating? or gambling?

6. Do I feel in control of these behaviors? Explain.

7. When you are in a bad mood I usually...
   - ☐ try to make you feel better
   - ☐ feel bad
   - ☐ fix it
   - ☐ offer to listen
   - ☐ ignore you
   - ☐ give you your space

29

NOTE: This page is reproduced from the Couple's Book.

8. Do I think that I am responsible for your feelings?

9. Am I concerned about your use of drugs or alcohol? spending? sexual activity? eating? or gambling?

10. Have I ever felt that any of these behaviors is out of control in your life? Explain.

11. Do I feel that we need to discuss the use of these substances or these behaviors? Why?

12. What would be acceptable drinking behavior in our home? Check all that apply.
   ☐ beer   ☐ hard liquor   ☐ wine
   ☐ daily   ☐ once a week   ☐ several a week
   ☐ several a month   ☐ on special occasions   ☐ never

13. Are either of us seeking professional help? If not, do I think that we should be?

14. How aware are we of the risk of AIDS infection from multiple sex partners and intravenous drug use? Have we discussed this? Why? Why not?

30

NOTE: This page is reproduced from the Couple's Book.

Her Page

Answer these questions by yourself. When you are finished discuss your answers and reflections with your partner.

1. Do I feel that you are trying to change me? How?

2. How do I think that our personalities complement each other?

3. How do I feel about discussing my past relationships? Can I be honest? Do I think that you really listen to me and understand?

4. How do I feel about discussing your past relationships?

5. Am I concerned about my use of drugs or alcohol? spending habits? sexual activity? eating? or gambling?

6. Do I feel in control of these behaviors? Explain.

7. When you are in a bad mood I usually...
   - ☐ try to make you feel better   ☐ fix it   ☐ ignore you
   - ☐ feel bad   ☐ offer to listen   ☐ give you your space

31

NOTE: This page is reproduced from the Couple's Book.

8. Do I think that I am responsible for your feelings?

9. Am I concerned about your use of drugs or alcohol? spending? sexual activity? eating? or gambling?

10. Have I ever felt that any of these behaviors is out of control in your life? Explain.

11. Do I feel that we need to discuss the use of these substances or these behaviors? Why?

12. What would be acceptable drinking behavior in our home? Check all that apply.
    ☐ beer   ☐ hard liquor   ☐ wine
    ☐ daily   ☐ once a week   ☐ several a week
    ☐ several a month   ☐ on special occasions ☐ never

13. Are either of us seeking professional help? If not, do I think that we should be?

14. How aware are we of the risk of AIDS infection from multiple sex partners and intravenous drug use? Have we discussed this? Why? Why not?

NOTE: This page is reproduced from the Couple's Book.

Issues of Special Focus

If these issues pertain to you, discuss them with your partner.

1. Do I want you to meet or know my ex-spouse?

2. Am I able to share with you the "story" of my previous marriage, and the reason(s) for the breakup?

3. In what ways is the personality of my (our) children different from my personality? Your personality?

4. Are you aware of anyone in your family who has been mentally ill? Have you shared this with your partner?

Relationship Check

Each of you should circle the number that best represents how you feel about your relationship after discussing this topic. Remember, you each need to select your own number.

1. very close   2. somewhat close   3. somewhat distant   4. very distant

What do I want to discuss further with you?

DUAL CAREER COUPLES

You may have heard of "DINK" couples. DINK stands for "dual income, no kids." Young, newly married DINK couples are becoming the norm in our society today. It sounds great, doesn't it? Double the income, few restraints (like kids)…and a life of fast food, long hours at work, and a messy apartment or house awaiting you at the end of the day. You see, having two jobs is great, but it also demands of you an even higher level of communication and effort to make the several elements of your life work together.

If you will both work, ask yourselves the following questions: Who will clean the house? pay the bills? vacuum and mop? take out the trash? cut the grass? stay home for the repairman? prepare the dinner? do dishes, laundry, grocery shopping? fix the leaky faucet? clean the bathtub, toilet, and bathroom?

Unfortunately, the traditional beliefs and behaviors of men and women in two-job marriages do not change just because both work outside the home. Studies show that women still do the majority of household chores regardless of the number of hours they spend at work. The entrenched perspective of the wife as homemaker still lingers in dual-career marriages. And the result could very well be a burned-out wife.

To help dual-career couples manage household chores, a graduate student at Southwest Texas State University developed a five-step approach. The following steps are intended to be done together.

STEP 1: Formulate a list of household chores.

STEP 2: Determine frequency of the tasks (daily, bi-weekly, etc.)

STEP 3: Agree on who is responsible to do the task: a) Consider each of your abilities and interests. b) Rotate the highly desirable or highly undesirable tasks.

STEP 4: Periodically review the chores to determine: a) Did the person designated do the task? b) Was it done to the satisfaction of both of you? c) If "no" is the answer to a or b, what prevented the completion of the chore? d) What more is needed (time, money, people) to get the chore done well?

STEP 5: Recycle: Add or drop chores, or change person responsible if necessary.

---

1. Discuss how each of you feels about who will do the chores in your house. Do you feel that men have certain tasks and women others? If your ideas are different from each other, how will you reach a compromise on chores?

2. Will both partners work if possible? How will this change, or not, when you have children?

3. What is more important to you in a job: the amount of money earned or the level of job satisfaction? Talk about your feelings about this with your partner. Do you agree on priorities in relationship to your job/career?

33

NOTE: This page is reproduced from the Couple's Book.

Two Different Directions

Marriage is the joining of two unique individuals coming together from "two different directions." The challenge that every couple faces is how to blend these different directions to form one shared journey.

They say they love each other
I've no doubt they do
They say they'll always be together
That may not be true

They come from different places
Different points of view
They find themselves in different spaces
Everything is all brand new

Two different directions
Too many different ways
One always on the road somewhere
The other one always stays
Too often unhappy
Too often on your own
When you are moving in different directions
True love is all alone

Old stories start to surface
Patterns from long ago
And loving quickly turns to anger
For reasons they don't even know

The strongest heart can be broken
With one insensitive word
The deepest feelings remain unspoken
No one is seen and nothing heard

NOTE: This page is reproduced from the Couple's Book.

Too different directions
Too many different ways
One always wants to work things out
The other one wants to play
Too ready for changes
Too much that just can't wait
When you are moving in different directions
True love can turn to hate

If opposites attract each other
What's the reason for
One being like an open window
One just like closing a door

Two different directions
Too many different ways
One likes to see the morning sunrise
The other one sleeps in late
Too many tomorrows
Too many times too late
When you are moving in different directions
True love may have to wait
If you are committed to different directions
True love will have to wait

Lyrics by John Denver

NOTE: This page is reproduced from the Couple's Book.

Our Family of Origin

Family systems therapy is a rapidly growing field in mental health. Based upon systems theory, it examines the way an individual interacts within his or her family and environment. All of us are members of several systems at the same time. Although we each influence these systems, they in turn also influence each of us.

The most influential system in anyone's life is their family of origin. The "family system" acts like a machine, with numerous gears and cogs all rotating against each other. What affects one member, affects the whole system, and vice versa. This chapter helps the engaged individual look at his or her family of origin as a system of interrelating parts so that he or she will begin to notice the parts and how they fit together. The engaged couple will find these exercises fun and challenging.

Although there are several exercises in the couple's workbook, we are including one more here in the leader's edition. The Family Roadmap, as you can see, is not in the couple's edition.

Distribute copies of this exercise if time permits in your marriage preparation program schedule. It needs to be monitored though, and should not just be handed out for the couples to take home and do on their own. You'll need to make sure that there is

paper for the couples to draw on and that each person has a copy of the Family Roadmap directions and model (this page is "photo-ready" in this volume).

With this exercise and all the exercises in this chapter, please heed the following warnings:

1. This is not therapy, and you are not therapists. Stress to the couples that the exercises in this chapter are for increased awareness and discovery. The results will undoubtedly be a renewed appreciation for certain parts of their upbringing, and a questioning of the value of certain other parts.

2. Avoid any hint of family bashing, that is, the tendency to lay blame for all problems on the family of origin. The point of this chapter is to start the individual looking to their family as a possible source of insights and/or answers for questions they may have about themselves. An individual or couple may choose later to pursue professional counseling to deal with past issues. However, be clear about your intention with this exercise: it is educative and not therapeutic!

3. Be alert for the individual or couple who may show signs of stress or negative emotional

reaction to any of these exercises. They may need or want help. If this happens, your response should be to approach the individual or couple gently, during the break or after the session or program, and offer a referral to several recommended professional counselors, or to your diocesan Catholic social agency.

This is a delicate matter that needs to be evaluated and handled carefully, but it should be a team decision. As an individual team couple you may want to "rescue" an apparently hurting individual, but you may do more harm than good if you act alone. Talk to the other team members first and the priest/minister. Compare observations and recommendations. You may find that your observations are not supported by the other members. But if, as a team, you do decide that a particular individual or couple is upset or having problems, one of the team members should approach them at an appropriate time and offer counseling referrals. This approach should be gentle and quick. No "saving" or "rescuing," no "Lone Ranger" heroism. If the couple or individual wants professional counseling, it is their responsibility to get it.

The Family Roadmap: Directions and Model

A family roadmap, also known as a genogram, is like a family tree, except that it also includes how members relate to each other. A family roadmap is helpful in enabling an individual to see how his or her family of origin has developed and is developing. It gives a person a sense of one's roots. It is quite involved and will take a while to complete.

Using the symbols, and the example on page 23, draw your family of origin roadmap. Start off by drawing either a square (for men) or a circle (for women) at the bottom of the page. Write your name below it and your age inside. Then proceed by working backward to any previous marriage or other serious relationship you've had; any children; your brothers or sisters; and finally to your parent(s). You may also choose to go a step beyond that and include your grandparents. Write down names, ages, and any brief, pertinent information next to each square or circle.

When you're done, place your roadmap next to your partner's and draw a line between the woman's circle and the man's square. This combined family roadmap is now the roadmap that leads to your marriage! And it will be the family roadmap for any children you have.

The family roadmaps below, for Fred and Bev, reveal interesting relationships in their families of origin. You may want to discuss this imaginary couple's roadmap in your small group, or just refer to it as a model for doing your own family roadmap.

A Family Roadmap

SYMBOLS

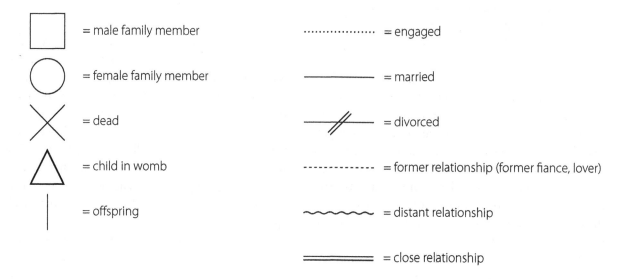

- □ = male family member
- ○ = female family member
- ✕ = dead
- △ = child in womb
- | = offspring

- ⋯⋯⋯ = engaged
- ——— = married
- ⟋⟋ = divorced
- - - - - = former relationship (former fiance, lover)
- 〜〜〜 = distant relationship
- ═══ = close relationship

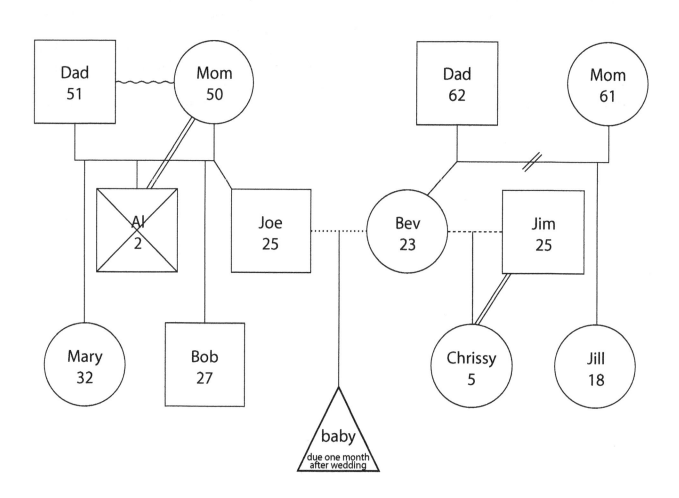

Notes

Our Family of Origin

Carol cannot stand the way Ron chews his food. She accuses him of sounding like a cow.

Maria is totally bewildered by Hector's intense dislike of her holding onto his arm when they're in public.

Jonathan and Kate constantly argue over the proper place in the kitchen for the salt and pepper shakers—in the cabinet or on the table?

Tyrone is confused about why Leslie exploded and admonished him when he affectionately patted her on the bottom.

Bob cannot stand to receive any advice, from anybody, at any time. His wife, Pat, loves to seek out the suggestions of others.

Luis has no qualms about taking a few "leeways" in filling out their income tax form. Ida has a strict belief in always doing what is right, and thinks such a practice is dishonest.

Have you ever been at a loss to explain the seemingly peculiar actions, thoughts, feelings, behaviors, or likes/dislikes of your partner? Do you find yourself sometimes insisting on something because it's "common sense"?

Do you sometimes find yourself wondering why you behave or feel or think the way you do?

Many times our view of the world around us, our perceptions of our partner's actions and words, or even our consideration of what's "logical" or "normal" is the result of being raised in a particular family. Our family of origin influences each of us far more than we are usually aware. Your feelings, your moods, your views of life, your sense of what is right and wrong, your internal sense of what's important and what isn't, all of this

NOTE: This page is reproduced from the Couple's Book.

has been largely shaped by your family of origin. Even your idiosyncrasies may be the result of the home in which you were raised.

Poor Ron doesn't realize that the reason Carol accuses him of sounding like a cow when he chews his food is because she grew up sitting at the dinner table with her dad chewing his food with great gusto . . . and noise! Unfortunately, Carol also probably doesn't realize that that's the reason herself. All she knows is that she feels guilty and confused when she snaps at Ron.

Your family of origin is the family with whom you were raised. This may be a home with two, one, or no parents. It may include 12 siblings, or you as an only child. It may also have included grandparents. Whatever the make-up was, your family of origin is/was exactly what the name implies: the family from which you originated. The key players obviously are your parent(s). They were your first teachers, role models, and significant persons in your life.

For some people, the words "mom" and/or "dad" conjure up feelings of warmth, love, and care. For others, the feelings are anger and hurt. And for most people, there is a mixture of good and bad feelings associated with "mom" and "dad." Whatever your feelings are, one thing is for sure: these feelings and the experiences associated with them will affect your new marriage and new family!

Your "new" family is you and your partner and any children either of you may have. Once you are married, you are family. And the families from which each of you came become your families of origin.

A good way to visualize how your family of origin has influenced who you are today is to imagine that through all your years of growing up you were packing your suitcase for a long vacation away from mom and dad. The type of clothes you pack, what seems important to you to take on this long vacation, what seems unimportant, all represent the values, behaviors, thoughts, feelings, and idiosyncrasies that you bring to your marriage. We all bring our luggage full of old family "stuff" to our marriages. And then often, sad to say, we spend the rest of our lives carrying that luggage around, guarding the contents as if it were priceless jewels, revealing only parts of it to our partners in defensive ways. We continuously seem to be amazed that we each have different "stuff" in our luggage, some of which is beautiful and worth keeping, and some of which is harmful and should be discarded.

MOVING BACK IN WITH PARENTS

Back when our country was young, several generations of the same family lived together under one roof. With the Industrial Era, twentieth-century families became more fragmented. The American Dream was, and still is, to own your own house and move out of Mom and Dad's.

Today, many young couples find themselves moving back in with Mom and/or Dad. Financial considerations are usually the reason for such a move, although the need to live separately before marriage is also a concern in many cases. Whatever the circumstances, preparations should be made in order for an easy and smooth adjustment for all involved in such an arrangement.

Multigenerational homes are becoming more common. So whether you are young and moving back home—either as an engaged individual or as a couple moving in with parents—or you are an older couple with an elderly and/or infirmed parent moving in with you, a few simple tasks may help prevent hard feelings or stresses down the road.

1. Sit down and talk with your parents. What are their expectations of living with you? Express your desires.

2. Mutually establish some basic ground rules with your parents in regard to privacy, responsibilities, rights, and financial considerations.

3. Mutually establish a timeline, if possible. If you are moving in with them, when will you be moving out?

4. If you need to continue living with your parents, sit down and discuss on a regular basis how the living arrangements are working out. What adjustments need to be made? What rules are working well? Which need to be changed?

5. Respect each other's "space"! Just because you live with your parents, don't assume they can drop everything just to pick you up at the service station.

37

NOTE: This page is reproduced from the Couple's Book.

IN-LAWS AND OUTLAWS

"United we stand, divided we fall!" Thus exclaimed one newly married couple, whose quasi-militant approach to in-laws was the result of constant parental meddling. Another couple described their relationship to both sets of parents as "fantastic, loving and close." What is your relationship to your parents? How about your future in-laws? Here are a few quick points to ponder when dealing with parents and in-laws:

1. Once the two of you marry, whether you have children or not, you are family.

2. Your parents will always be your parents, but once your are married, your primary relationship is to your spouse.

3. Love your parents, and show them the respect they deserve.

4. But establish right away, some clear boundaries between you, as a couple, and your parents.

There needs to be an emotional, psychological, and physical border made between your new family (you and your partner) and your families of origin. If you are emotionally or mentally "enmeshed" with your parents, you will not be able to establish your own separate identity, traditions, rituals, and way of doing things. And this could lead to some serious problems down the road.

Your partner is marrying you, not your family. As we read in Paul's letter to the Ephesians (5:31): "For this reason a man [a woman] will leave his [her] father and mother and be joined to his wife [her husband], and the two will become one flesh." In order to unite as one, you each must first truly leave home.

We believe that it is important for each of you to sit down and open up your luggage now, and share the "stuff" inside, before you marry. The questions in this chapter will help you do that. There may be quite a few surprises, and it also may be a painful experience. Sharing who we truly are is never an easy task, even when it's with the one we love.

An important topic for each of you to look at and share is family of origin "rules." What were the "dos" and "don'ts" in the home in which you grew up? Some rules may be easy to remember because they were obvious rules, like "We all go to church every Sunday," or rules regarding homework or chores. Other rules, however, may have been more hidden or subconscious. These are the unspoken rules, like "We don't cry in this family," or "We don't show emotions," or "Don't hang your 'dirty laundry' out for the neighbors to see." The identification and naming of the parental rules under which you grew is important, because these rules, especially the hidden, unspoken ones, are the rules under which you probably still function today as an adult. And they may be harmful to your marriage and your own emotional well-being.

Think back to your childhood. What were the rules of the house? Focus on the unspoken rules, the ones which everyone knew but never talked about. This is hard to do, but nonetheless important. Usually the hidden rules of a family are based on how members should feel, think, behave, and cope with problems, and are typically "don't" rules.

Henry, the adult child of an alcoholic mother, was able to identify the "hidden rules" in his family. Very simply, they were: "You don't express feelings; You cope with problems by rationalizing them away; You always act as if life is great even when at home Mom is drinking." By naming these unspoken rules out loud, and then realizing how destructive they were to his own marriage, Henry was better able to deal with his wife, his children, and his own feelings.

These "hidden rules" of your family of origin have a life of their own. And, to return to the analogy of the vacation, they often sneak into your luggage without your knowing. You didn't consciously put them in, but they're there. And they are destructive!

In this chapter, you will find several exercises and questions that address the issue of family of origin. As with all the chapters in this workbook, you may not get to finish all the items contained here during your marriage preparation program. How-

38

NOTE: This page is reproduced from the Couple's Book.

ever, we strongly encourage you to finish all the exercises and questions in this chapter on your own, and to return to them throughout your marriage.

Your marriage is truly a journey. Know what "stuff" is in the luggage you're bringing with you!

A.C.O.A.

The phrase "Adult Children of Alcoholics" (A.C.O.A.), or simply "adult children," refers to the grown offspring of alcoholic parents who, as a result of being raised in a dysfunctional family, have acquired unhealthy feelings, traits, behaviors, values and/or thinking that ultimately takes away from their quality of life. ACOAs usually suffer from co-dependency (see information box on page 22). And, to make matters worse, ACOAs tend to marry alcoholics, addicts, or other ACOAs, thus perpetuating their own unhealthy co-dependency.

Often ACOAs are not fully aware of how destructive some of their behavior and thinking is. Deep down they know "something's not right," but they try to suppress what they're feeling in hopes that the "hurt" of growing up in an alcoholic home will go away. It won't. Not by itself.

If you or your partner grew up in a home where alcohol or drugs were regularly abused, chances are you're an ACOA. And if you are, you need a counselor to help you work through some of your feelings. It's not easy. But the alternative is worse: the alternative is an unhappy life.

See the Resource Appendix for information about national ACOA groups.

NOTE: This page is reproduced from the Couple's Book.

DINNER WITH THE _____

(Fill in your family name)

This exercise will require some time, quiet, and imagination. Whether you do this "imagery" exercise during a marriage preparation program or on your own, try to find some space by yourself to allow you to really get into it.

Visualize what a typical dinner time looked like in your family of origin when you were about 10 years old. Describe it to your partner by answering some or all of the following questions.

- Where is the dinner? (dining room? kitchen? in front of the TV? at a restaurant?)

- What are you eating?

- Who's present?

- Where does everyone sit in relation to one another?

- How do you, as a 10 year old, feel?

- Who's absent?

- Why are they absent?

- What's the topic(s) of conversation?

- Who does the talking?

- Who does the listening?

- What will each person do after dinner?

NOTE: This page is reproduced from the Couple's Book.

His Page
How "healthy" was your family of origin?

In **Traits of a Healthy Family**, *Dolores Curran names fifteen traits that "healthy families" have in common, chosen by over five hundred family health professionals, including priests, ministers, counselors, teachers, and social workers.*

You will find these fifteen traits of healthy families listed below. Read over each one and consider how it applies to your family of origin as you were growing up. For example, for the first trait ask yourself, "How well did my family of origin communicate and listen?" And then rate each trait by circling a number from 1 to 5 (1 = did not do well, 5 = did very well). When you're done, draw a line connecting all your circles and go through your ratings with your partner, and discuss them.

A healthy family...	My family of origin...				
...communicates and listens.	1	2	3	4	5
...affirms and supports one another.	1	2	3	4	5
...teaches respect for others.	1	2	3	4	5
...develops a sense of trust.	1	2	3	4	5
...has a sense of play and humor.	1	2	3	4	5
...exhibits a sense of shared responsibility.	1	2	3	4	5
...teaches a sense of right and wrong.	1	2	3	4	5
...has a strong sense of family in which rituals and traditions abound.	1	2	3	4	5
...has a balance of interaction among members.	1	2	3	4	5
...has a shared religious core.	1	2	3	4	5
...respects the privacy of one another.	1	2	3	4	5
...values service to others.	1	2	3	4	5
...fosters family table time and conversation.	1	2	3	4	5
...shares leisure time.	1	2	3	4	5
...admits to and seeks help with problems.	1	2	3	4	5

41

NOTE: This page is reproduced from the Couple's Book.

Answer the following questions and then discuss them with your partner.

1. What are three strengths in my family of origin?

2. What are three areas in which my family of origin was not strong?

3. What traits and/or idiosyncrasies do I see in you that I also see in your parent(s)?

4. What traits and/or idiosyncrasies do I see in you that I also see in my own mother/father?

5. How close was my family when I was growing up?

   1. very close   2. somewhat close   3. somewhat distant   4. very distant

6. When I was growing up, who did the household chores? (Create a list of chores and assign them to your mother and father as you remember each. Discuss with your partner which of you will be responsible for the chores on your list.)

42

NOTE: This page is reproduced from the Couple's Book.

Her Page
How "healthy" was your family of origin?

*In **Traits of a Healthy Family**, Dolores Curran names fifteen traits that "healthy families" have in common, chosen by over five hundred family health professionals, including priests, ministers, counselors, teachers, and social workers.*

You will find these fifteen traits of healthy families listed below. Read over each one and consider how it applies to your family of origin as you were growing up. For example, for the first trait ask yourself, "How well did my family of origin communicate and listen?" And then rate each trait by circling a number from 1 to 5 (1 = did not do well, 5 = did very well). When you're done, draw a line connecting all your circles and go through your ratings with your partner, and discuss them.

A healthy family...	My family of origin...				
...communicates and listens.	1	2	3	4	5
...affirms and supports one another.	1	2	3	4	5
...teaches respect for others.	1	2	3	4	5
...develops a sense of trust.	1	2	3	4	5
...has a sense of play and humor.	1	2	3	4	5
...exhibits a sense of shared responsibility.	1	2	3	4	5
...teaches a sense of right and wrong.	1	2	3	4	5
...has a strong sense of family in which rituals and traditions abound.	1	2	3	4	5
...has a balance of interaction among members.	1	2	3	4	5
...has a shared religious core.	1	2	3	4	5
...respects the privacy of one another.	1	2	3	4	5
...values service to others.	1	2	3	4	5
...fosters family table time and conversation.	1	2	3	4	5
...shares leisure time.	1	2	3	4	5
...admits to and seeks help with problems.	1	2	3	4	5

43

NOTE: This page is reproduced from the Couple's Book.

Answer the following questions and then discuss them with your partner.

1. What are three strengths in my family of origin?

2. What are three areas in which my family of origin was not strong?

3. What traits and/or idiosyncrasies do I see in you that I also see in your parent(s)?

4. What traits and/or idiosyncrasies do I see in you that I also see in my own mother/father?

5. How close was my family when I was growing up?

   1. very close   2. somewhat close   3. somewhat distant   4. very distant

6. When I was growing up, who did the household chores? (Create a list of chores and assign them to your mother and father as you remember each. Discuss with your partner which of you will be responsible for the chores on your list.)

44

NOTE: This page is reproduced from the Couple's Book.

Issues of Special Focus

If these issues pertain to you, discuss them with your partner.

1. If one or both of you have children from a previous relationship, describe the family of origin of your child's other parent as best you can. Reflect on the questions and apply the exercises in this chapter.

2. If your parents have died, are there any unfinished, unsettled arguments or unspoken conversations that you wish you could have had, or completed with them? If so, write your parent(s) a letter and tell them what you would have wanted to say. Hold on to the letter and share it with your partner someday when you are ready.

3. If you were abused as a child, have you told your partner? Have you gone for counseling? If not, why?

Group Section

Discuss this case study as a group. Answer the following questions.

1. What do you think Maggie and Jeff need to look at regarding their families of origin?

2. What do each of them need to do?

Relationship Check

Each of you should circle the number that best represents how you feel about your relationship after discussing this topic. Remember, you each need to select your own number.

1. very close   2. somewhat close   3. somewhat distant   4. very distant

What would I want to discuss further with you?

CASE STUDY

MAGGIE AND JEFF

Maggie's eyes were filling with tears as she told the counselor of the problems she and Jeff were experiencing in their young marriage. Maggie likes to visit her parents often. They only live ten minutes away, and especially with her mother's recent illness, she feels a need to spend time with them.

Jeff doesn't like the idea that she's over there almost every day. The visits aren't always long, although she's been known to spend the entire evening there. It frustrates Jeff that she's always "running home to mommy and daddy."

Maggie was raised in a large, tight-knit family. She lived with her parents, whom she adored, right up to her marriage at the age of 23. Her father earned a good living and retired at an early age. Her mother was a dedicated, traditional wife and mother who managed the home well.

Jeff and his two younger brothers were raised by his father. His mother died when Jeff was nine. And although he gets along fine with this father, there is a "distance" there. Jeff's father had to be both mom and dad to his sons, which was difficult considering he held down two jobs most of his life. Jeff's strict paternal grandparents, who were from Germany, helped the father raise the boys. But basically Jeff and his brothers grew up taking care of themselves. Their father was affectionate when he was home. And he was careful to tell the boys stories of their mother, lest they forget her.

Jeff looks at the counselor and says, "I don't know what's wrong with my wanting Maggie to spend less time with her parents and more time with me." Maggie, looking hurt, responds, "I am able to spend a little time with my folks and still have plenty of time for Jeff." The counselor recommends that they look at their families of origin to uncover some of their problems.

45

NOTE: This page is reproduced from the Couple's Book.

Our Sexuality

The issues of sexuality and sex may be difficult for the engaged couple to address. Interestingly, in working with engaged couples we have found that there is often a mental chasm between what a couple thinks they know and what they really do know about sexuality. In other words, many couples think they pretty well know everything there is to know about sex and sexuality. This may be because their perspective is a more biological, action-focused one. Of course, as a team couple, you will not address the issue with the same perspective. The perspective of sexuality and sex revealed in this chapter focuses on personal relationships. A couple may feel that they are good at sex. But are they good at being well-rounded, loving sexual partners? There's a difference!

The engaged couples are presented with a wholistic perspective of sexuality and are challenged to look inside themselves for both the masculine and feminine traits in each of us. In presenting a talk on sexuality, you may want to consider taking our analogy of a diamond and elaborate on the many facets there are to the sexuality of a married couple. Nothing beats a good visual prop in a talk: bring in a large crystal dangling from a string and hold it up as you make the analogy.

Gender-specific roles is an important and lively issue these days. Are men to do only the "manly" jobs around the house? What about the "feminine" chores? Why the distinction? This whole topic is excellent for small group discussion, and will probably flow right out of the roles/traits exercise listed in the Group Section of the couple's edition.

The concluding paragraphs of this chapter look at sex as a beautiful, delicate gift from God. This perspective, held up against the backdrop of societal views of sex that often abuses it in advertising, entertainment, or money-making, is a refreshing alternative for most couples. We are all inundated with an endless flood of negative and unhealthy messages regarding sex, whether from television, magazines, movies, friends, the workplace, or school. This chapter holds out a powerful message for an engaged couple when they witness married couples who present sex as a God-given, holy form of communication between a husband and wife. It shatters the view of contemporary society.

Our Sexuality
Talk Outline

1. Introduce self and topic
- Number of years married?
- Any children? Ages?
- Town you live in? Church?
- How long involved as marriage preparation volunteer couple?
- Any other general information about yourselves?
- What's your topic?
- Why is it important for them, as engaged couples, to hear about this topic?

2. "Sexuality" is a word most of us equate with "sex"
- This is both unfortunate and incorrect.
- Actually sexuality refers to who you are as a person, and it includes your personality, beliefs, gender, feelings, behaviors, physical body, and ability to relate to others, to name a few.
- You are a sexual person, at *all* times, in *all* situations, not just when sex is involved.
- Sexuality involves how you feel about yourself—your self-image, self-esteem, and self-love.
- Feeling that you are unlovable and unattractive to your partner will adversely affect your marriage.

3. Feminine and masculine traits are in *each* of us
- Men will favor the masculine. Women will favor the feminine.
- The more you can balance the two, the healthier a person, and the better marriage partner you will be—and *the happier you'll be.*
- Traits of Feminine vs Masculine:

gentle	assertive
process-oriented	goal-oriented
feelings	thoughts
emotion	logic

- Both sets of traits are good. The important thing is balance between the two.

4. "Feminization" of marital relationship
- The traits listed as feminine are those that enhance the marital relationship.
- Those listed as masculine inhibit good communication and the sharing of self and feelings.
- The more feminine traits in your marriage and in your communication, the healthier your relationship.

5. Influences on our sexuality
- *Family of Origin.* Our parents defined for us as we were growing up what it meant to be a woman and a wife, by watching mom, and what it meant to be a man and a husband, by watching dad.
- *Social pressures.* Our society defines what it means to be a "real man" or a "real woman." Certain expectations are put upon us in order to be accepted in our culture.
- *Media.* Movies, advertisements, and other media define male and female behaviors. Whether we like it or not, they influence us.
- *Church.* Church teachings define Christian women and men, as well as set up acceptable behaviors and manners of living.

6. As a Christian couple, we see our sexuality and sexual expression as good and as a gift from God

- Believe that our bodies are good, as able to comfort, care for and please each other.
- See intercourse as a special gift that strengthens our relationship, deepens our communication and intimacy, heals and comforts us, points to the fidelity of our marriage and the exclusiveness of our sexual expression.
- Our sexual expression offers us gifts and opportunities: to new life in our relationship, healing, renewing and nurturing our love, and to new life in the decision to have a child.

7. Having a child is a decision

- Demands honest communication about fears, feelings, and doubts.
- Need to discuss how many? when? finances? careers? day care? infertility? adoption? no children?

8. Need to challenge couples to keep their love life alive as they would any other form of communication

NOTES:

1. Read the couple's and leader's edition chapters on this topic.
2. Lace this and all talks with personal stories, examples, and anecdotes that add color and/or demonstrate what you are talking about.

Notes

Our Sexuality

Y ou may think, "Now comes the good part of the book...sex!" Well we hate to disappoint you, but the topic of this chapter is sexuality, and not just sex. While sexuality includes sex, it also includes much more.

Your sexuality is who you are as a person. It refers to you as a man or a woman. Now that you're engaged, this becomes more important than ever because you are going to have to help your partner understand what it means to live intimately with you. You probably think you know each other pretty well. But occasionally there will be things about each of you that will still surprise the other. No matter how long you have known each other or been married, there are still new things to discover about yourselves. And this only adds richness to your relationship.

Some of these new discoveries can be attributed to personality, some to education, some to how you were raised, and some just to your own likes and dislikes. But all of these surprises and unique little things are part of you as a sexual human being. Your sexuality permeates everything about you.

Such a holistic perspective should free you from some false assumptions and societal expectations. One such myth says that manhood or womanhood is linked to a person's ability to perform sex. This myth ignores the fact that you are a sexual person at all times, in all situations. Your masculinity and femininity are expressed in countless ways every day, and not only in bed.

As a sexual being, you are like a diamond. You're one of a kind. You're

NOTE: This page is reproduced from the Couple's Book.

beautiful and priceless to your partner. And, like a diamond, there are many facets to you as a sexual human being.

The first two facets of your sexuality are the feminine and masculine traits found in each of us. Men typically stress the masculine, and women the feminine. However, everyone needs to accept and use both masculine and feminine traits. In other words, women need to be in touch with and express their masculine side, and men their feminine side.

Some of the traits associated with our feminine side include nurturing, affection, compassion, sympathy, tenderness, understanding, gentleness, and an orientation toward feelings, people, and relationships. Those associated with the masculine side include protecting, ambition, dominance, self-reliance, forcefulness, aggression, and an orientation toward thoughts and things.

A healthy person embraces the traits from both. To be a complete and balanced person, it is necessary for women to be assertive and confident and for men to be tender and nurturing! Refusing to acknowledge these traits can cause problems in your relationship and hinder true communication. This sense of balance also extends into all areas of your relationship: your intimacy, role identification, and lovemaking.

Another facet of your sexuality is intimacy, or the sharing of yourself with your partner in a focused, exclusive way. This is when we allow our partner to see who we really are, to share ourselves without defenses or pretenses. Intimacy is the glue that holds it all together. A lack of intimacy is often the cause of problems for a couple.

A couple came to see us complaining that the romance was gone. She was too tired and he too bored with the routine of their lovemaking so they just gave it up. When we talked about the other areas of their life—job, children, home life, we discovered they were so busy they didn't have time to talk to each other until 11:00 P.M. each night, at which time they tried to settle the day's activities with the kids, the bills, and their responsibilities to other family members. No wonder the romance was gone! After a few weeks of getting more time together to focus on their relationship and settling the big family issues earlier in the day, they discovered that their sex life wasn't really gone after all. Intimacy in their communication renewed the intimacy in their lovemaking.

But how do you become intimate in your communication? It strikes us that men and women do communicate differently about close interpersonal relations, as the following lists show:

SEXUAL ADDICTION

Just as an alcoholic has a pathological addiction to alcohol, a sex addict has a pathological addiction to sex and unhealthy relationships. According to a brochure published by the Golden Valley Health Center, Minneapolis, "Sexual addiction or dependency is defined as engaging in obsessive/compulsive sexual behaviors which cause severe stress for the individual and his/her family. The addicted person is unable to control his/her behaviors and lives in constant fear of discovery."

Sexual addicts might engage in or use chronic masturbation, pornography, prostitution, might cultivate compulsive heterosexual or homosexual relationships, exhibitionism or voyeurism, might frequent "adult" book stores, might engage in anonymous sex, indecent phone calls, child molestation, incest, and rape. The addictive behavior becomes increasingly uncontrollable and ultimately destructive for the addict and those close to him/her.

Being a sex addict is more than being "a jock" or "a tease," and it's definitely not a joke. For more information, see the resource appendix at the end of this workbook.

NOTE: This page is reproduced from the Couple's Book.

Qualities of Female Communication

Focus on the process
Sensitive, feeling
Sharing
Confront and settle issues
Give and take
Express
Assertive
Compassionate
Gentle

Qualities of Male Communication

Focus on the results
Keep to the facts
Logical
Avoid issues
Who's right?
Suppress
Aggressive
Analytical
Dominant

Although each approach to communication has its merits and deficiencies, the female qualities listed above tend to improve intimacy in couple communication better than do the male qualities. This feminization of marital communication, when talking with the one you love, invites us to be sensitive, sharing, expressive, compassionate, and gentle. This, of course, is not a hard, fast rule. There are times when you need to stick to the facts, reach a conclusion quickly, and be logical. But generally speaking, the more gentle you can be with each other, the more intimate your communication will be.

Another facet of your sexuality as husband and wife will include role identification and who will do what around the house. Traditionally, household chores have been gender-specific. Wives do certain jobs because these jobs are considered feminine, and husbands perform the masculine jobs. However, over the past thirty years there has emerged a more egalitarian approach toward household tasks. In such a model, the couple looks at each of their individual strengths, likes, and dislikes, and then mutually decides who should do what. We recommend that you follow such an egalitarian approach in divvying up household chores. It further enhances couple communica-

---

INFERTILITY

The U.S. Public Health Service estimates that approximately 25 percent of married couples experience long-term fertility problems. They cannot conceive a child at all, or they cannot have as many as they'd like.

Infertility is not an uncommon problem for couples. And yet when a couple experiences difficulty or inability to conceive a child, they often feel isolated and alone. "Everyone else can have a baby, why can't we?"

Infertility may be connected to male impotence, low sperm count, sterility or defective sperm or egg production as the result of infectious diseases, blocked Fallopian tubes, or various other reasons.

Fertility should not be perceived in relation to manhood or womanhood. But unfortunately this false connection is made, especially by men. Virility and fertility are seen as synonymous. Fertility problems are not connected to how much of a man or woman you are. Fertility problems are not rare. And fertility problems should not be kept a secret or kept in the dark. The more you seek professional advice, and confide in trusted friends or family, the more you'll realize how common it is.

Consult a physician if you think you are infertile. There are a variety of methods of treatment that work well.

48

NOTE: This page is reproduced from the Couple's Book.

tion and ultimately provides the most satisfaction to each of you.

When we moved to a new house several years ago, it was a common sight every Saturday morning to see husbands out cutting the grass. However, because of work and school responsibilities, John wasn't able to do much of the grass mowing. Consequently, Sue was typically out there every weekend, cutting the grass with all the husbands. After several weeks of humorous little comments from the neighbors regarding our nontraditional ways, we noticed that some of the other women started cutting the grass. By the end of the summer, it was mostly the women pushing the mowers every weekend. Where were the men? We were almost afraid to ask, but we hope they were inside doing the laundry or changing the baby!

The final facet of your sexuality is sex. Physical sharing of yourself with your partner is one of the most intimate forms of communication in your relationship. It is here that you give yourself to your partner physically, emotionally, psychologically, and spiritually. And it is in the giving and receiving of each other that lovemaking can be mutually life-giving and satisfying.

Sex is a gift given by a good God to a loving couple. It possesses, beyond all other communications, the unique power to create new life in the couple's relationship as well as in the form of a child. It is here in its potential to create that we are privileged to glimpse the handiwork of God in our relationships.

Most of us have been influenced by the ideas that sex and God were separate and that somehow sex or things of the body were shameful. We have also witnessed a society that flaunts and abuses sex and the body through pornography and promiscuity. While these ideas about sex may have influenced us, we need not accept them.

Our lovemaking and sexuality are gifts to us from a loving Creater, to be nurtured lovingly. Handle them gently and your marriage will grow and blossom.

AIDS

AIDS does not discriminate. By now, each of us has probably known someone who has been positive for HIV, the virus that causes AIDS. We have learned that HIV can be transmitted in a number of different ways: through contact with body fluids such as blood, semen, vaginal secretions, and saliva; through the sharing of needles; with the reception of blood transfusions; and through sexual contact.

At first, this disease was more prominent among gay men and intravenous drug users. It has, however, extended into the heterosexual community, infecting males as well as females, adults as well as adolescents. And HIV has infected infants born to mothers with HIV and/or AIDS.

HIV and AIDS are everyone's concern. If you have had multiple sex partners or have been an intravenous drug user, please get tested. It only takes one time and one contact to become infected—and to infect your loved one, as well.

AIDS is a reality which we all need to be informed about. You will be affected by AIDS whether it be through a family member, friend, co-worker, or neighbor. If you don't know much about this disease, please educate yourself. (See the resource appendix at the end of this book for the phone number of the AIDS hotline sponsored by the Centers for Disease Control.)

49

NOTE: This page is reproduced from the Couple's Book.

NATURAL FAMILY PLANNING

Natural Family Planning (NFP) refers to several methods of avoiding or achieving pregnancy that cooperate with a couples' own natural fertility. Unlike artificial birth control, which suppresses a couple's natural fertility by means of drugs or contraceptive devices, NFP is 100 percent natural.

Natural Family Planning is not to be confused with the old calendar "rhythm" method, which often proved to be unreliable. Unlike rhythm, which simply used mathematical calendar calculations to predict ovulation, NFP is based on the observation of the fertile and infertile periods of a woman's cycle. Couples abstain from intercourse during the fertile phase of the cycle if they are using NFP to avoid pregnancy. For couples who are finding it difficult to conceive a child, NFP is helpful in its emphasis on fertility awareness.

Natural Family Planning is morally acceptable to all religions, and is in harmony with the official teaching of the Catholic church, which prohibits any means of artificial contraception.

There are two commonly used NFP methods: the Ovulation Method and the Sympto-Thermal Method. Both are very reliable and effective. Instruction by a qualified teacher is essential with NFP. Contact your church or diocese to find out more information and when classes are held, or the national office for Natural Family Planning (see resource appendix).

For more information, we recommend the following publications:

The Art of Natural Family Planning, John and Sheila Kippley (Couple to Couple League, 1996).

The Billings Method, Dr. Evelyn Billings and Ann Westmore (New York: Ballantine Books, 1997).

You can also contact these NFP organizations for resources and publications:

Couple to Couple League
John Kippley, President
PO Box 111184
Cincinnati, OH 45211-1184
(513) 471-2000
FAX: (513) 557-2449

Family of the Americas Foundation
Mercedes Wilson, Executive Director
PO Box 1170
Dunkirk, MD 20754
(301) 627-3346
FAX: (301) 627-0847

Northwest Family Services
Rose Fuller, Executive Director
4805 NE Glisan Street
Portland, OR 97213-2957
(503) 215-6377
FAX: (503) 215-6940

**Pope Paul VI Institute for the
Study of Human Reproduction**
Thomas Hilgers, MD, Executive Director
6901 Mercy Road
Omaha, NE 68106
(402) 390-6600
FAX: (402) 390-9851

NOTE: This page is reproduced from the Couple's Book.

His Page

1. How comfortable am I in discussing sex with you? (*Circle one.*)
   How comfortable are you? (*Put an X on one.*)

         1. very uncomfortable   2. somewhat uncomfortable

         3. somewhat comfortable   4. very comfortable

2. On a scale if 1 to 5 (5 = highest), how affectionate do I think you are? (*Circle one.*)
   How affectionate do I wish you would be? (*Put an X on one.*)

               1   2   3   4   5

3. What do I find most physically attractive about you?

4. What do I think is my most physically attractive feature?

5. In my family of origin: sex was… (*check as many as appropriate*)

   ☐ never discussed   ☐ viewed as a gift from God   ☐ openly talked about

   ☐ the focus of many jokes   ☐ considered "dirty"   ☐ other_____

6. True or False: T   F

             ☐   ☐   To me, sex is extremely important.

             ☐   ☐   To you, sex is extremely important.

             ☐   ☐   Once we are married, I have a right to your body.

             ☐   ☐   If I'm angry at you, I have a right to withhold sex.

             ☐   ☐   Romance comes naturally.

             ☐   ☐   If you cheated on me I would end our marriage.

7. Once we are married, do I think that I will be able to initiate our lovemaking, or will I wait until you do?

8. Will I be able to say "no"? How will I feel if you say "no"?

51

NOTE: This page is reproduced from the Couple's Book.

9. If I was sexually abused or raped as a child or adult, have I talked with you about it? Have I sought counseling?

10. Have we discussed any past sexual relationships? Did the discussion affect our relationship? How?

11. Am I aware of ever having been at risk for contracting HIV?

12. Have I ever been tested for the AIDS virus? Have you?
Have we discussed this? Is this something that I think that we need to talk more about?

13. How do I feel about sex outside of marriage?

14. Are there any sexual acts within marriage that I will find unacceptable? What?

15. In our everyday dealings with each other, I wish you would be: (*check all that apply*)
- ☐ more gentle
- ☐ stronger
- ☐ more expressive with your emotions
- ☐ more independent
- ☐ more caring
- ☐ more open with your thoughts
- ☐ less emotional
- ☐ less demanding
- ☐ more attentive to my needs
- ☐ more willing to negotiate
- ☐ less hesitant to make decisions

16. Have we talked about family planning and birth control? What have we decided? Who made the decision?

17. Have I ever participated in any of the following? Have you? (*check all that apply*)
- ☐ voyeurism (peeping tom)
- ☐ exhibitionism
- ☐ massage parlors
- ☐ pedophilia (sex with children)
- ☐ adult book stores
- ☐ incestuous relations
- ☐ anonymous sex (sex with strangers)
- ☐ prostitution (sex for pay)

18. If our sex life was in trouble, would I want us to seek counseling? Do I think that you would agree to it?

19. Is there anything about sex that I want to ask or talk about with someone other than you?

52

NOTE: This page is reproduced from the Couple's Book.

Her Page

1. How comfortable am I in discussing sex with you? (*Circle one.*)
   How comfortable are you? (*Put an X on one.*)

          1. very uncomfortable   2. somewhat uncomfortable

          3. somewhat comfortable   4. very comfortable

2. On a scale if 1 to 5 (5 = highest), how affectionate do I think you are? (*Circle one.*)
   How affectionate do I wish you would be? (*Put an X on one.*)

                1   2   3   4   5

3. What do I find most physically attractive about you?

4. What do I think is my most physically attractive feature?

5. In my family of origin: sex was… (*check as many as appropriate*)

   ☐ never discussed   ☐ viewed as a gift from God   ☐ openly talked about

   ☐ the focus of many jokes   ☐ considered "dirty"   ☐ other_____

6. True or False: T   F

                    ☐   ☐   To me, sex is extremely important.

                    ☐   ☐   To you, sex is extremely important.

                    ☐   ☐   Once we are married, I have a right to your body.

                    ☐   ☐   If I'm angry at you, I have a right to withhold sex.

                    ☐   ☐   Romance comes naturally.

                    ☐   ☐   If you cheated on me I would end our marriage.

7. Once we are married, do I think that I will be able to initiate our lovemaking, or will I wait until you do?

8. Will I be able to say "no"? How will I feel if you say "no"?

53

NOTE: This page is reproduced from the Couple's Book.

9. If I was sexually abused or raped as a child or adult, have I talked with you about it? Have I sought counseling?

10. Have we discussed any past sexual relationships? Did the discussion affect our relationship? How?

11. Am I aware of ever having been at risk for contracting HIV?

12. Have I ever been tested for the AIDS virus? Have you?
Have we discussed this? Is this something that I think that we need to talk more about?

13. How do I feel about sex outside of marriage?

14. Are there any sexual acts within marriage that I will find unacceptable? What?

15. In our everyday dealings with each other, I wish you would be: (check all that apply)
   ☐ more gentle   ☐ stronger   ☐ more expressive with your emotions
   ☐ more independent   ☐ more caring   ☐ more open with your thoughts
   ☐ less emotional   ☐ less demanding   ☐ more attentive to my needs
   ☐ more willing to negotiate   ☐ less hesitant to make decisions

16. Have we talked about family planning and birth control? What have we decided? Who made the decision?

17. Have I ever participated in any of the following? Have you? (check all that apply)
   ☐ voyeurism (peeping tom)   ☐ exhibitionism   ☐ massage parlors
   ☐ pedophilia (sex with children)   ☐ adult book stores   ☐ incestuous relations
   ☐ anonymous sex (sex with strangers)   ☐ prostitution (sex for pay)

18. If our sex life was in trouble, would I want us to seek counseling? Do I think that you would agree to it?

19. Is there anything about sex that I want to ask or talk about with someone other than you?

54

NOTE: This page is reproduced from the Couple's Book.

Group Section

Answer the following questions alone, then as a couple, and then discuss your answers with other couples.

1. Which roles or traits listed below do you, as a couple, believe should be associated with men, women, or both? (Mark with an M for Men. Mark with a W for Women. Mark with a B for Both.)

_____ dominant	_____ protective	_____ aggressive	_____ soft spoken
_____ nurturing	_____ precise	_____ provider	_____ patient
_____ compassionate	_____ works part-time	_____ disciplines kids	_____ writes letters
_____ homemaker	_____ works full-time	_____ plans vacations	_____ does grocery shopping
_____ takes garbage out	_____ changes diapers	_____ creative	_____ pays bills
_____ loving	_____ leader	_____ dependent	_____ expressive
_____ distant	_____ cuts grass	_____ loud	_____ healer
_____ gentle	_____ independent	_____ passive	_____ works on cars
_____ does dishes	_____ cooks	_____ active	_____ emotional
_____ strong	_____ weak	_____ breadwinner	_____ cleans
_____ does banking	_____ does laundry	_____ vacuums	_____ follower

2. If you were to explain sexuality and sex to your child, what would you want them to know? Why? What would you not tell him or her?

Issues of Special Focus

If you or your partner was abused as a child:

1. If I was abused as a child, have I been able to talk about it with you? Do I think that you understand?

2. If your partner was abused as a child, is there anything that you want to discuss with him/her about the past?

3. Do you ever feel that the past abuse interferes with your present relationship? How?

If these issues pertain to you, discuss them with your partner:

1. As a couple with a great age difference, how will our sex life be affected in the years to come?

2. How will our children from past relationships affect our sex life? Family planning? Privacy?

Relationship Check

Each of you should circle the number that best represents how you feel about your relationship after discussing this topic. Remember, you each need to select your own number.

1. very close   2. somewhat close   3. somewhat distant   4. very distant

What would I want to discuss further with you?

55

NOTE: This page is reproduced from the Couple's Book.

Our Children

"Do you want to have children?"

"Oh yes, we'd love to have a baby!"

"No, I asked whether you want to have children. They're only babies for a short time. But they'll be your children all your life."

This conversation between an older married couple and a young engaged couple continued with a discussion about the responsibilities and hardships, and the joys and thrills involved in raising children. The engaged couple quickly caught on: deciding whether to have children, when, and how many is a life-altering decision. It's not a difficult concept to understand and yet many young couples without children do not realize it unless it's pointed out to them.

Young couples who are expecting or planning to have a child will usually plan the nursery well, buy all the necessary blankets, clothes, toys, and maybe even look ahead to start a college fund. However, few young couples are prepared for the day-to-day challenges of being a parent. "Once you're a parent, you're always a parent!"

One big turn-off for young couples is an older couple who smiles that all-knowing smile, and enunciates little pearls of wisdom such as, "Just you wait and see!" or "Oh my God, wait until you have children!" or "Enjoy yourselves now, 'cause once you have children...." Please don't speak to a young couple in that vein. It's better to speak of the love, satisfaction, and joy involved in watching children grow than of the personal hardships and difficulties you have had in raising them. We typically say something like, "We absolutely love being a mother and father....But having children has changed our lives very much." The engaged couple usually gets the picture.

An engaged couple should discuss in detail the timing and number of children. If you encounter a couple who hasn't talked about it at all or who seem to think having children is "no big deal," talk to them earnestly! Don't give them any pearls of wisdom—just speak from the heart.

Notes

CHAPTER SIX

Our Children

A t a recent marriage preparation program, an engaged couple approached us during one of the refreshment breaks. Our topic was children and parenting, and some of what we said had obviously struck a nerve with this couple. They were an attractive, intelligent couple in love, but they had a major problem. They explained that they were to be married in two months, and that they disagreed on the issue of children. He wanted one, possibly two, in four or five years. She wanted a lot of children, and wanted to start right away. They had discussed it at length, and were still unable to resolve the issue. We tried to put their dilemma into some perspective.

Several years ago, Sue was counseling a married couple in their early 40s. Their problem as they presented it was their sexual relationship. However, after several sessions, the real problem surfaced. They had been married for 15 years and had never settled their dilemma regarding children. Like the engaged couple above, this couple had disagreed on the number and timing of children. They hadn't addressed the issue in detail before they married. And after their wedding, the issue became so heated that their marriage almost ended in divorce after only one year. The fact that they had only one child was not the result of an agreed upon family plan. Rather, because of the unresolved issue, they rarely made love.

We had no simple answer for that engaged couple at the marriage preparation program. But we did emphasize that they had to resolve the problem before they married. And the answer had to be one that they each agreed to and could live with, without resentment.

56

NOTE: This page is reproduced from the Couple's Book.

You and your partner must also address, in detail, the number and timing of children before you begin your marriage. If one or both of you have children already, do not assume that you agree on the prospects of having a child together in the future.

We waited four years before we had our first child. We had discussed this at length before our wedding and had come to an agreement. Interestingly enough, we changed our minds after we married but still were in agreement. It was as if our initial groundwork in communicating on family planning had given us the right tools to continually dialogue and revise our plans along the way.

The night before Justin was born, we were sitting on the floor in the newly painted nursery reflecting upon our first four years of marriage, and wondering what it would be like to no longer be a twosome. With some sadness we realized that our lives were about to change dramatically. We felt a sense of hope and a sense of loss. We knew that one stage of our relationship was about to end, and a new one to begin. We had an overwhelming sense of "passage," as if we were about to walk through a one-way door. Looking back we're amazed at how accurate our feelings were. Having a child is definitely a one-way passage. After this, your life is never the same.

Just as it takes two of you to conceive a child, it takes two of you to raise a child. Mothers as well as fathers need to take responsibility for the nurturing, loving, and disciplining. For your children's sake, each of you has to supply plenty of time together, hugs, kisses, and appropriate discipline. And please notice we use the term "discipline" and not "punishment." Discipline, which comes from the same word as disciple, refers to educating and guiding your child. Punishment is negative, abusive, and counterproductive to raising a healthy, loving child.

Consider how you were raised. If you were abused physically, sexually, emotionally, or spiritually, you will have a greater tendency to similarly mistreat your offspring. If you were an abused child, we strongly recommend that you seek professional counseling. Seeing a counselor is a sign of health and is the mature thing to do for yourself, your spouse, and your children.

As an engaged couple, what should you consider in your discussion about having and raising children? Part of that discussion should include the impact that the birth of a child will have on your job(s) and, more importantly, how your jobs may affect your children. Too often, one partner assumes that the other will stop working, put a career on hold, and stay home with the

AND BABY MAKES...?

In spite of the fact that more couples today are choosing to remain childless, the overall expectation of society is that a young couple will eventually, if not right away, have children. Having children is expected. It's seen as the norm. Often the phrase "starting a family" is used. This is unfortunate because you started your family the day you married. A childless couple is a family.

But, will you have children? What are your reasons? If any of the following reasons seem good to you, then think again!

1. "My (our) parents would die if we didn't."

2. "Why not? All my friends are having babies."

3. "Babies are so cute… I want one!"

4. "Having a baby will strengthen (save) our marriage."

5. "It's sort of expected; besides, it won't change our relationship that much."

6. "I want to stay home and not work."

7. "I want a baby to give me an identity. To make me feel important."

The following are some good reasons for wanting a child.

1. "As mature adults, we are deciding to have a baby and to assume all the responsibilities associated with it."

2. "Our relationship is sound and our love is secure; we want to raise a child in our warm, nurturing home."

3. "We are looking forward to rearing a child from birth to adulthood."

4. "We have so much love to give."

5. "I am psychologically and emotionally mature enough to be a parent to a baby who will be totally dependent on me."

The effect children have on marriage is tremendous! A baby can bring unbelievable joy, and frustration, to a couple. Parenting is an experience of both agony and ecstasy…ask any parent!

57

NOTE: This page is reproduced from the Couple's Book.

MISCARRIAGES AND STILLBIRTHS

For those women and couples who experience a miscarriage or a stillbirth, the sense of loss and sorrow can range from mild to devastating. Approximately one of four pregnancies will result in miscarriage or stillbirth. Women over 35, and those who smoke, drink alcohol, or do drugs are more likely to miscarry. After twenty weeks of pregnancy the spontaneous natural termination of the fetus' life is referred to as a stillbirth, and no longer technically as a miscarriage.

But more important than these facts on miscarriage and stillbirth are the feelings associated. For some reason, in the general consciousness of society there is a lack of understanding and empathy for those who have experienced such a loss. People tend to minimize it. Family and friends have been know to make idiotic and heartless statements such as: "Don't worry, you can try again," or "Who are we to question God's plans?"

For those who have experienced a miscarriage or stillbirth, especially couples who are trying to have a child, the grieving for the unborn baby is very real and very normal. The prospects of having another child are no consolation at the time. And family and friends can help the most by offering the couple a shoulder to cry on, an ear to listen, and a hand to hold.

baby. Assuming rather than talking it out usually develops into a problem.

Explore your options, be honest with each other, and make your decision together. You may want to start off by discussing your responses to the following: Which of us wants to stay home? Which of us wants to work outside the home? Is part-time work an option? What child care options do we have? What do I feel is best for our children? Remember too that the decision you make as a couple can be adapted and changed as time goes by and the number or ages of the children change.

Acknowledge, too, that just because you're biologically equipped to produce a child does not mean you are emotionally, spiritually, and developmentally ready to be a mom or a dad. Being a good parent requires neither a Ph.D. in child psychology nor memorization of one of the many child care books on the market. It does require some more basic things: maturity, a capacity to love and to be loved, a commitment to your marriage and to your children. Bringing a child into the world is a decision that you as a couple should make together. Some couples will decide to wait, while others may decide to have a child early in their marriage. And still other couples may decide for very good reasons not to bring a child into the world at all.

Finally, being a good parent embraces a sense of "the spiritual" in all life. A child is not just flesh and bones, but a person, separate from its mother and father. Each child is a unique creation of God, an awesome symbol that life and love should continue. In the process of bringing new life into the world, we enter into the realm of the divine. We become co-creators with God, a role that should not be taken lightly.

NOTE: *This page is reproduced from the Couple's Book.*

His Page

1. Do I want to have children? If so, how many? If not, why?

2. How long do I want to wait until we have a baby?

3. Do I think I would be/am a good parent? Explain:

4. As a parent, I will emphasize and/or supply the following for our children.
   (*Pick 4 and number in order, 1 = highest priority*)

   ___ college fund(s)   ___ a love of life   ___ good education
   ___ church attendance   ___ discipline   ___ whatever they want
   ___ self-respect   ___ love of God   ___ the latest clothes
   ___ fear of God   ___ respect for others   ___ lots of fun times
   ___ toys   ___ a sense of right/wrong
   ___ plenty of hugs/kisses ___ respect for environment

5. I think having children will change/impact our marriage (*Circle*):

   not at all   some   significantly

6. What's my main reason for wanting a child?

7. How would I respond if our baby was born with physical or mental problems?

8. True or False:

T F
☐ ☐ We both have to discipline our children.
☐ ☐ Having a baby can help a marriage in trouble.
☐ ☐ Our children will have to adapt to our life-style.
☐ ☐ Spanking is good for a child.
☐ ☐ Our baby will always be the center of our lives.
☐ ☐ Feeling loved is one of life's greatest gifts.

T F
☐ ☐ Family planning is the woman's responsibility.
☐ ☐ Children are a gift from God.
☐ ☐ In an unwanted pregnancy, I'd consider abortion.
☐ ☐ Our children will probably be put in day care.
☐ ☐ It's primarily up to the mother to care for the children.

59

NOTE: This page is reproduced from the Couple's Book.

9. Have we talked about family planning? What method of family planning/birth control do I foresee us using?

10. Who will be the primary care provider for our children during the day? me? you? grandparents? a neighbor or friend? a day-care center? other?

11. What effect will having a baby have on our income? our jobs?

12. If I had a choice between maintaining a certain level of income and lifestyle by keeping my job, or quitting my job so that I can stay home with our children, what would I choose?

13. If we discovered that one of us is infertile and we could not have our own biological children, I would feel...

14. How do I feel about adopting a child?

JEALOUSY

Love and jealousy are not the same. As Margaret Mead stated, "Jealousy is not a barometer by which the depth of love can be read. It merely records the degree of the lover's insecurity....It is a negative, miserable state of feeling having its origin in the sense of insecurity and inferiority."

We are all jealous at one time or another. But if it becomes an ongoing experience, there may be a problem. Continuing suspicious feelings about a partner's fidelity tend to create further suspicions. An irrational preoccupation with keeping watch on your partner is destructive.

Ongoing jealousy is based on a poor self-image. And it is also difficult to hide from others. Unfortunately, some individuals will actually attempt to make their partner jealous in order to test the relationship, get attention, or "get back at" him or her for some perceived crime.

What do you do if jealousy is a recurring presence in your relationship? Sit down and talk it out! Is one of you intentionally making the other jealous? Why? What makes one of you jealous? What can you do as a couple to alleviate the problem? And finally, if you are the jealous person, you may want to scrutinize your own level of security. If you have recurring strong feelings of jealousy, you may want to talk to a professional counselor.

60

NOTE: This page is reproduced from the Couple's Book.

Her Page

1. Do I want to have children? If so, how many? If not, why?

2. How long do I want to wait until we have a baby?

3. Do I think I would be/am a good parent? Explain:

4. As a parent, I will emphasize and/or supply the following for our children.
   (*Pick 4 and number in order, 1 = highest priority*)

   ___ college fund(s)   ___ a love of life   ___ good education

   ___ church attendance   ___ discipline   ___ whatever they want

   ___ self-respect   ___ love of God   ___ the latest clothes

   ___ fear of God   ___ respect for others   ___ lots of fun times

   ___ toys   ___ a sense of right/wrong

   ___ plenty of hugs/kisses ___ respect for environment

5. I think having children will change/impact our marriage (*Circle*):

   not at all   some   significantly

6. What's my main reason for wanting a child?

7. How would I respond if our baby was born with physical or mental problems?

8. True or False:

T F

☐ ☐ We both have to discipline our children.

☐ ☐ Having a baby can help a marriage in trouble.

☐ ☐ Our children will have to adapt to our life-style.

☐ ☐ Spanking is good for a child.

☐ ☐ Our baby will always be the center of our lives.

☐ ☐ Feeling loved is one of life's greatest gifts.

T F

☐ ☐ Family planning is the woman's responsibility.

☐ ☐ Children are a gift from God.

☐ ☐ In an unwanted pregnancy, I'd consider abortion.

☐ ☐ Our children will probably be put in day care.

☐ ☐ It's primarily up to the mother to care for the children.

61

NOTE: This page is reproduced from the Couple's Book.

9. Have we talked about family planning? What method of family planning/birth control do I foresee us using?

10. Who will be the primary care provider for our children during the day? me? you? grand-parents? a neighbor or friend? a day-care center? other?

11. What effect will having a baby have on our income? our jobs?

12. If I had a choice between maintaining a certain level of income and lifestyle by keeping my job, or quitting my job so that I can stay home with our children, what would I choose?

13. If we discovered that one of us is infertile and we could not have our own biological children, I would feel...

14. How do I feel about adopting a child?

JEALOUSY

Love and jealousy are not the same. As Margaret Mead stated, "Jealousy is not a barometer by which the depth of love can be read. It merely records the degree of the lover's insecurity....It is a negative, miserable state of feeling having its origin in the sense of insecurity and inferiority."

We are all jealous at one time or another. But if it becomes an ongoing experience, there may be a problem. Continuing suspicious feelings about a partner's fidelity tend to create further suspicions. An irrational preoccupation with keeping watch on your partner is destructive.

Ongoing jealousy is based on a poor self-image. And it is also difficult to hide from others. Unfortunately, some individuals will actually attempt to make their partner jealous in order to test the relationship, get attention, or "get back at" him or her for some perceived crime.

What do you do if jealousy is a recurring presence in your relationship? Sit down and talk it out! Is one of you intentionally making the other jealous? Why? What makes one of you jealous? What can you do as a couple to alleviate the problem? And finally, if you are the jealous person, you may want to scrutinize your own level of security. If you have recurring strong feelings of jealousy, you may want to talk to a professional counselor.

NOTE: This page is reproduced from the Couple's Book.

Group Section

"Baby" Cases: Discuss these case studies as a group, answering the questions at the end of each.

GINNY & WIL: Ginny and Wil waited seven years before they attempted to have a child. They're now in their mid-30s and have found that they are not able to have children. The resulting stress and anxiety has made them lash out at each other. They feel that their marriage may end. ***What do you think they need to do?***

BOB & NICKI: Since they brought her home from the hospital, Bob and Nicki's cute little bundle of joy has turned into a big bundle of "terror." Little Heather is colicky. She cries and screams throughout the night, every night. No one sleeps. The doctor says there's nothing they can do except "wait it out." But after very little sleep over several weeks, Bob is starting to stay late at work and Nicki is depressed and moody. ***What further problems may develop? What can they do? Make a list of suggestions.***

JEFF & ANN: Jeff and Ann have a strong marriage based on good communication skills. However, since they had Nathaniel, they find they're not communicating as well. Ann is angry that Jeff does not get more involved in caring for Nathaniel; Jeff is angry because of their sudden loss of freedom. And when they try to talk about their feelings, little Nathaniel cries, needs to be changed or fed. ***What can they do to improve their situation?***

MARY & LYLE: Lyle works at a factory and earns significantly less money than his wife, Mary, does as an executive secretary. They're planning on having a baby. And they agree that they don't want to put the baby in day care. Someone will have to stay home. But it would be difficult for them to live on Lyle's income alone. And yet, he feels strongly that he should continue working. After several fights on the subject, Mary's wondering if they'll ever have a baby at all! They've decided to see a marriage counselor. ***What do you think the marriage counselor will have them focus on? How would you handle the situation?***

YOUNG AND PREGNANT BEFORE THE WEDDING

We often think teenagers and young people in their early twenties feel indestructible. Even when they see their own friends die from drinking and driving, or become pregnant, or messed up with drugs, they often intuitively believe, "It can't happen to me."

Counselors refer to this feeling of indestructibility as a personal fable. In other words, it encompasses the false, unrealistic view about self that allows a young person to take risks.

People who become pregnant by accident are usually very aware of the risk of sexual intercourse, and yet still get pregnant. Why? They didn't think it could happen to them.

And yet, once they get pregnant, many feel marriage is the proper response, the honorable thing to do. This is in face of the fact that the highest divorce rate group is teenagers who marry when she's pregnant. In spite of the collapse of their personal fable (she is pregnant), they maintain another personal fable about being married happily ever after. When confronted with the overwhelming statistics of divorce and/or abuse in teenage pregnant marriages, a typical response is, "That won't happen to us, we're not a statistic."

A minister we know says he refuses to marry any pregnant teenage couple who comes to him until after the birth of the baby. Interestingly enough, he says, more than half of the couples never end up marrying. It seems a lot of such couples feel tremendous pressure, from parents predominantly, to get married. But once the baby comes, they realize that the world does not come to an end if there is no wedding.

So, if you're young, pregnant, and got engaged as a result, ask yourself: Why am I marrying? Is the answer based squarely on love, or on doing the honorable thing? Remember, two wrongs don't make a right.

63

NOTE: This page is reproduced from the Couple's Book.

Issues of Special Focus

If one or both of you are coming to this marriage with a child from a previous relationship:

1. Take turns and describe for each other how you each understand what the relationship will be between the new partner and the children.

2. How do the children feel about the marriage? How do they feel about the prospective partner?

3. What will you do if the children object to the marriage? How will you deal with the children?

4. Discuss how having a child will affect: privacy; your time together as a couple; freedom.

5. Have you talked about discipline? How will you resolve your differences? Can you agree on a method of discipline that is acceptable to both of you?

6. Discuss how the child's financial needs for clothes, activities, doctor's visits, school supplies, etc., will be met. Who will support the child?

If you or your partner was abused as a child:

1. Am I afraid that the abuse may be repeated with our child(ren)?

2. Make a list of things that you can do to avoid this. Include who you would talk to about it or where you could turn for help.

Relationship Check

Each of you should circle the number that best represents how you are feeling about your relationship after discussing this topic. Remember, you each need to select your own number.

| 1. very close | 2. somewhat close | 3. somewhat distant | 4. very distant |

What would I want to discuss further with you about this topic?

PREMARITAL COUNSELING

In many Catholic dioceses, and some Protestant churches, there are policies regarding premarital counseling or evaluation. Typically such policies stipulate that a couple must receive counseling and/or an evaluation prior to the wedding if certain conditions are present.

These conditions may include pregnancy, youth (the couple is under 18 years of age), immaturity, or any other pastoral concern that the priest or minister may have about the couple's readiness for marriage. The purpose of premarital counseling is to help couples with special circumstances or problems to see more clearly some difficulties that may lie ahead, and to equip them better to make a mature Christian decision regarding their relationship. Like marriage preparation itself, premarital counseling is an opportunity for growth and enrichment.

NOTE: This page is reproduced from the Couple's Book.

Our Finances, Friends, Work, and Leisure Time

"Finances, friends, and fun—yes, I'd like all three, please." Unfortunately, all three can grow into problems for a married couple if they don't communicate about them. This chapter ties in the three areas, touching also on jobs and careers, and challenges the couple to be specific in their expectations.

The budget worksheet is a favorite exercise among engaged couples. Before they get into it though, stress that the process of budget planning is just as important as the end result. In other words, how they communicate and treat each other during the budget planning is just as important as the budget itself.

It is suggested that team members go to banks and insurance agents and obtain brochures and other forms of information on renter's insurance, homeowner's insurance, auto and life insurance, various savings and checking accounts, I.R.A.s, C.D.s, and other annuities and funds. Place these on a table so the couples can take what they want during a break in the program.

In speaking on finances, shy away from the nuts and bolts of finances, and stick more to the interpersonal, relational aspects on how to communicate on finances. In your group of engaged couples you may have a 35-year-old C.P.A. sitting next to an 18-year-old secretarial student who doesn't know how to write a check. You can't meet all the needs of such a wide range of experience. And yet they all have one common need: to hear a married couple talk about how they handle finances in their relationship. Success is not determined by the amount of money made, but by how the marriage is strengthened and communication increased.

Friends and the use of leisure time is sometimes a sore issue for couples. Anyone who's worked with engaged couples has heard one partner complain about the other's friends, or the boys-night out, or the lack of fun time they spend with each other. We may be tempted to discount or minimalize such complaints from the engaged. Don't! If they're having a hard time now with their separate friends and the use of, or lack of, leisure time, then how will it change once they are married? It may get worse. They need to discuss all this thoroughly, to the satisfaction of each. You can help by encouraging them to stay focused on it and not to trivialize the topic themselves through jokes or silence.

Our Finances, Friends, Work, and Leisure Time

Talk Outline

1. Introduce self and topic

- Number of years married?
- Any children? Ages?
- Town you live in? Church?
- How long involved as a marriage preparation volunteer couple?
- Any other general information about yourselves?
- What's your topic?
- Why is it important for them, as engaged couples, to hear about this topic?

2. The A–B–C–D of handling finances (without ruining your marriage)

- *A=Appreciation!* of what you have materially, of what income you have, and of each other. It's fine to have future goals and to improve your standard of living. However, don't forget to be thankful for what you have *now*—enjoy life now!
- *B=Budget!* List out sources of income vs debt/expenses. Refer to budget planner in engaged couple's workbook.
- *C=Communication!* Practice good communication skills when discussing finances. Listen to each other. Work as a team, not as opponents.
- *D=Discipline!* Both partners have to understand and be committed to working through financial matters. Both have to be willing to sacrifice, share and/or surrender one's "wants" in order to pay for our "needs." (NOTE: You may consider presenting these in reverse order, D–C–B–A.)

3. Insurance: health, major medical, life, dental, auto, home, or renter's. Discuss these at length. For example:

- *Health.* Essential. Typically a benefit offered by an employer.
- *Major medical.* Same as health.
- *Life.* Not essential, but highly advisable especially if you have or are expecting children. Along this topic, consider having wills drawn up by an attorney. Some see this as morbid, others see it as "peace of mind." Usually young couples do not see a need for wills. Suggest that they are worth more than they think.
- *Dental.* Nice benefit from employer if offered, but not necessary.
- *Auto.* Check the requirements of the state you live in. Discuss the necessary coverages.

4. Credit. Discuss the appeal of credit cards and "no payment until June" loans and the financial consequences

5. Charity and stewardship. Discuss the importance of giving to those who are in greater need than we are and of supporting our parish community

NOTES:

1. Read the couple's and leader's edition chapters on this topic.
2. Lace this and all talks with personal stories, examples, and anecdotes that add color and/or demonstrate what you are talking about.

Notes

CHAPTER SEVEN

Our Finances, Friends, Work, and Leisure Time

Did you ever play with a mobile? The one hanging above the crib in our house has mesmerized two babies with its bright colors and delicately balanced animals. Touch one of the animals and all of them move. What affects one, affects the whole. How like a mobile are your marriage and the other dimensions of your life! Your marital relationship is the hub, from which grows your career, your finances, your leisure activities, your intimate time together as a couple, your other relationships, your children, and your time alone. They're all connected. What affects one affects the whole system. Too much, or not enough time and energy placed in one area will disturb the whole system and negatively affect other elements of your marriage.

Like a mobile, your marriage should dance with a beautiful balance when touched on one side, maintaining the balance even during the dance. This chapter will deal with four elements of your life that directly affect your relationship which, if not handled well, may destabilize your marriage. How well your marriage "balances" depends in part on how you deal with money, how the work and play of your lives mesh, and how you involve both friends and family in your life.

For many couples finances are an area of conflict. Although making a lot of money may make life easier, not making a lot of money is rarely the actual cause for conflict. Rather, conflict arises over how couples manage their money. Different expectations, assumptions, and priorities lead to different styles of fiscal management. We recommend two basic things: First, have a budget. Agree on it and stick to it! Second, communicate with

65

NOTE: This page is reproduced from the Couple's Book.

MR. MOM

Today in the United States more men are assuming the role of homemaker, primary childcare provider, or "domestic engineer." According to the Bureau of Labor Statistics, in 2006 over 159,000 husbands stay home to care for the kids while the wives work outside the home. Economic opportunity for the family, career opportunity for the wife, and the desire of fathers to care for their children full time are typically the guiding force behind the growth in the number of "Mr. Moms."

The U.S. census bureau reports that the fastest growing segment of the workforce today is married mothers of young children. The wife may be able to earn significantly more than the husband, and thus will find herself kissing both hubby and baby good-bye in the morning as she heads for the office.

Men are finding that they can be the primary caregiving parent and not relinquish any sense of masculinity or self-worth. And, in fact, those daddies who do stay home with young children typically find it a nurturing and enriching experience.

Regardless of who assumes the role of primary childcare provider, studies show that there is a trend in the U.S. for both parents to be actively involved in the raising of children. And children whose fathers and mothers are equally involved in all aspects tend to grow up more self-confident and emotionally and psychologically well adjusted.

each other about your budget, your finances, your worries, and your hopes.

It never ceases to amaze us how couples fail to communicate on this topic. We've known couples who don't even know what each partner makes in salary! Others divide their money between "his" and "hers" with no allotment for "ours." One such couple took turns purchasing the common major items they needed, which resulted in a house furnished with "her" couch, "his" TV, "her" end tables, "his" coffee table, "her" kitchen table, and so on. Their reasoning: if they divorce, it'll be easy to figure out who gets what!

Typically, couples with few problems based on money are those who have a healthy, on-going line of communication. They have joint accounts and each partner knows what's coming in and going out. Each may take a different role such as bill payer, salary check depositor, banker, and/or checkbook balancer, but they keep each other informed. One does not make major purchases without the agreement of the other.

Good communication helps couples "balance" work and play as well. Until recently, the prevailing work ethic emphasized work over leisure. Being with your family and having fun were granted the time that was "left over" from one's true purpose in life: to work!

A recent trend in career counseling reflects more current attempts to view our lives as a whole, made up of many parts. Career counselors advise job seekers to consider all aspects of their lives, work play, family, and friends when choosing or changing a career. The premise is that your career (loosely defined as the type of work you pursue) should be a part of your overall lifestyle. Thirty years ago, marriages and families had to conform to the husband's job. Today, couples are rightfully seeking careers that harmoniously connect with their private family lives.

These ideas are reflected in our attempts to achieve a "balance" of work and play in our lives. Some people have no problem playing and may need to concentrate more on work. Others, regulated by the "work ethic," need to learn the value of play and spontaneity! Marriages, new and old, need humor, playfulness, laughter, dancing, joking. Choosing a particular career or re-evaluating the one you already have can create more time to spend with your partner, adding new and life-giving experiences to your relationship.

Your relationship with your friends will probably change once you are married, especially if they are not married. While

66

NOTE: This page is reproduced from the Couple's Book.

old friends aren't dropped just because you marry, some become "our" friends once they get to know you as a couple, and others may naturally fade away. You may also find that some do remain "his" or "her" friends and are, along with the other kinds of friendships, life-giving and not destructive to your relationship. An occasional "boys' night out" or "girls' night out" is fine, but not on a regular basis. This may be a difficult adjustment at first, but it's a necessary change for the long-term health of your marriage.

Many couples marry because they get along, find each other attractive and interesting, and "can live with each other." But when they need to talk about something important, they turn to a friend for support. Eventually these couples find they are out of touch and have grown apart. We believe that husbands and wives need to be best friends, able to communicate about all facets of their lives so that, like the mobile, the individual gifts each brings to the marriage achieve the rhythm and grace of elements that work well together.

BALANCING FAMILY AND WORK

Since the start of the industrial revolution some 250 years ago, our society fell into a pattern of seeing the husband as the "bread-winner" for the family and the wife as the "homemaker." Currently, however, many, if not most, women are working outside the home, and many families rely on the income from both spouses to get by.

The emotional transition in all this hasn't come as swiftly as the employment transition. Many married women working outside the home speak of the challenge of trying to meet both work and family obligations, and the stress and guilt that can arise when trying to find the balance. Studies often show that husbands are getting better at helping around the house, but that these duties still fall disproportionately on wives. And women who choose the more traditional homemaker role sometimes feel as if society is treating them as if they aren't very valuable.

As a couple about to marry, it is very important that you discuss your work and family expectations—for how you balance work and family will greatly affect your marriage.

NOTE: This page is reproduced from the Couple's Book.

His Page

Answer these questions by yourself and then share your answers with your partner.

1. In what ways is money a source of conflict for us? What would I like to change?

2. Who managed the money in my family of origin?

3. What, if any, concerns do I have about how you spend money?

4. My chief goal for five years from now

5. My "ideal" house is

6. What, if any, concerns do I have about any of your friends or mine?

7. Am I content with how we spend our free time? What would I change?

8. My "ideal" vacation is

9. Am I content with how our jobs/careers affect our relationship? Why?

69

NOTE: This page is reproduced from the Couple's Book.

His Financial Worksheet

Complete this worksheet by yourself. Discuss your answers with your partner, and then together complete "Our Financial Worksheet."

1. What is our present combined monthly net income? $_____

2. What are our combined present assets? $_____
   _____checking account(s)   _____real estate (house, condo, townhouse, etc.)
   _____saving account(s)   _____clothing
   _____C.D.s/stocks/savings   _____jewelry
   _____cars/trucks/vans   _____furniture/appliance
   _____others: _____ ; _____ ; _____ ; _____

3. How much do I think we should spend a month on the following items?

Housing: $_____
_____mortgage/rent
_____insurance & tax
_____utilities & fuel
_____phone
_____maintenance/repairs
_____home decorating & miscellaneous

Transportation: $_____
_____car payments
_____insurance & taxes
_____gas & maintenance
_____repairs
_____public transportation

Food: $_____
_____groceries
_____liquor, beer
_____tobacco

Clothing & Personal Care: $_____
_____his
_____hers
_____kids
_____cosmetics, haircuts, etc.

Fun & Leisure: $_____
_____eating out
_____movies/videos
hobbies
_____sports events

Insurance: $_____
_____medical/hospitalization
_____life insurance
_____retirement

Charges, Loans, Installments, Miscellaneous: $_____
_____furniture   _____credit cards   _____educational loans/expenses
_____wedding rings   _____pets   _____donations & charity
_____alimony/child care _____savings   _____memberships/subscriptions
                                              _____other: _____

4. *Total Monthly Expenses:* _____ vs *Total Monthly Income:* _____

_____
70

NOTE: This page is reproduced from the Couple's Book.

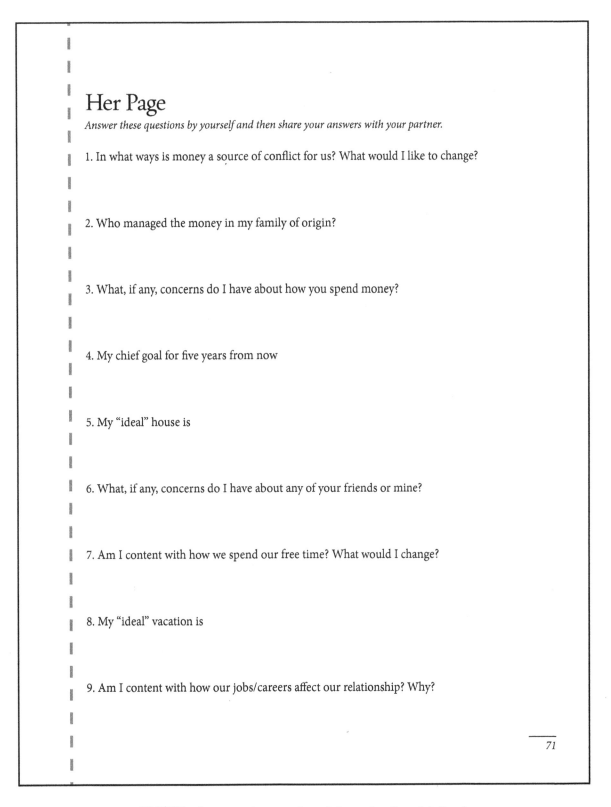

Her Page

Answer these questions by yourself and then share your answers with your partner.

1. In what ways is money a source of conflict for us? What would I like to change?

2. Who managed the money in my family of origin?

3. What, if any, concerns do I have about how you spend money?

4. My chief goal for five years from now

5. My "ideal" house is

6. What, if any, concerns do I have about any of your friends or mine?

7. Am I content with how we spend our free time? What would I change?

8. My "ideal" vacation is

9. Am I content with how our jobs/careers affect our relationship? Why?

71

NOTE: This page is reproduced from the Couple's Book.

Her Financial Worksheet

Complete this worksheet by yourself. Discuss your answers with your partner, and then together complete "Our Financial Worksheet."

1. What is our present combined monthly net income? $_____

2. What are our combined present assets? $_____
   _____checking account(s)   _____real estate (house, condo, townhouse, etc.)
   _____saving account(s)   _____clothing
   _____C.D.s/stocks/savings   _____jewelry
   _____cars/trucks/vans   _____furniture/appliance
   _____others: _____ ; _____ ; _____ ; _____

3. How much do I think we should spend a month on the following items?

Housing: $_____   *Transportation:* $_____
   _____mortgage/rent   _____car payments
   _____insurance & tax   _____insurance & taxes
   _____utilities & fuel   _____gas & maintenance
   _____phone   _____repairs
   _____maintenance/repairs   _____public transportation
   _____home decorating & miscellaneous

Food: $_____   *Clothing & Personal Care:* $_____
   _____groceries   _____his
   _____liquor, beer   _____hers
   _____tobacco   _____kids
                                        _____cosmetics, haircuts, etc.

Fun & Leisure: $_____   *Insurance:* $_____
   _____eating out   _____medical/hospitalization
   _____movies/videos   _____life insurance
   _____hobbies   _____retirement
   _____sports events

Charges, Loans, Installments, Miscellaneous: $_____
   _____furniture   _____credit cards   _____educational loans/expenses
   _____wedding rings   _____pets   _____donations & charity
   _____alimony/child care _____savings   _____memberships/subscriptions
                                                           _____other: _____

4. *Total Monthly Expenses:* _____   vs *Total Monthly Income:* _____

72

NOTE: This page is reproduced from the Couple's Book.

Our Financial Worksheet

After you have discussed your individual answers on the His & Her Worksheets, complete this worksheet as a couple. If you run into disagreements, don't worry. It may take a while before you can come to an agreement on some issues. Just remember to use good communication and fair fighting skills in your discussions!

What is our present combined monthly net income? $_____

What do we think we should spend monthly on the following items?

Housing: $_____
_____mortgage/rent
_____insurance & tax
_____utilities & fuel
_____phone
_____maintenance/repairs
_____home decorating & miscellaneous

Transportation: $_____
_____car payments
_____insurance & taxes
_____gas & maintenance
_____repairs
_____public transportation

Food: $_____
_____groceries
_____liquor, beer
_____tobacco

Clothing & Personal Care: $_____
_____his
_____hers
_____kids
_____cosmetics, haircuts, etc.

Fun & Leisure: $_____
_____eating out
_____movies/videos
_____hobbies
_____sports events

Insurance: $_____
_____medical/hospitalization
_____life insurance
_____retirement

Charges, Loans, Installments, Miscellaneous: $_____
_____furniture
_____wedding rings
_____alimony/child care

_____credit cards
_____pets
_____savings

_____educational loans/expenses
_____donations & charity
_____memberships/subscriptions
_____other: _____

Total Monthly Expenses: _____   vs *Total Monthly Income:* _____

1. Where were the areas of disagreement?
2. Where did you each need to compromise?
3. How do you feel about your financial situation?

73

NOTE: This page is reproduced from the Couple's Book.

Group Section

Discuss this case study with other couples in a small group.

Mark and Linda each hold a job, making a total of $80,000 a year. They live in a nice home with a combined monthly mortgage, taxes, and house insurance payments that eat up 33% of their take-home pay.

They charge purchases like household items, clothes, and electronic equipment and entertainment expenses, spending their cash on food and extras. They have 8 credit cards total. Savings and investments are a low priority for them.

1. What concerns do you have for Mark and Linda's financial situation?

2. What could be the potential dangers?

3. What changes would you suggest to them?

Issues of Special Focus

If these questions pertain to you, jot down your answers and discuss them with your partner.

1. If one or both of us were married before, what difficult situations may, or already have arisen concerning old friends from the previous marriage(s)? How will we handle such difficulties?

2. If one or both of us have children already, have we discussed how our new blended family will deal with tighter financial constraints?

3. If we're presently expecting a baby, how will we juggle childcare, our job(s), and financial demands?

Relationship Check

Each of you should circle the number that best represents how you are feeling about your relationship after discussing this topic. Remember, you each need to select your own number.

1. very close   2. somewhat close   3. somewhat distant   4. very distant

What might I want to discuss further with you about this topic? Discuss your individual answers.

NOTE: This page is reproduced from the Couple's Book.

Our Spirituality

Along with communication, spirituality is the most important topic for an engaged couple to discuss. It is not only an important topic, but a wide topic. It includes sacramentality, religion, faith, church, and personal beliefs—all of which are connected yet separate. It would take a separate workbook to cover all this in depth. In this chapter we try to cover all of it to various degrees. Lest you, a team member, become overwhelmed (and thus discouraged) by the breadth and depth of this topic, remember the following:

Just by the mere fact that you walk into the room as a married couple, obviously committed not only to your own marriage but also to the welfare of others, you have given the best lesson on couple spirituality to the engaged. Your participation as a married couple in the marriage preparation process provides a great witness for the engaged couples. As the authors of *Preparing For Marriage: A Study of Marriage Preparations in American Catholic Dioceses* (St. Meinrad, Ind.: Abbey Press, 1983) state: "[W]e found it reassuring that clergy and laity are working together in most marriage preparation programs. Couples are not only being prepared for marriage but are also being offered a model and an experience of church in the process."

This is why it is so important to have married couples run marriage preparation programs. The sign value is very great, indeed. Any couple's marriage is a journey of faith, a journey that begins with the preparation process. Ideally, a couple will grow spiritually during this brief process. In their statement *Faithful to Each Other Forever: A Catholic Handbook of Pastoral Help for Marriage Preparation*, the U.S. bishops affirmed that one of the goals of marriage preparation should be "the identification and deepening of the couple's faith." You help facilitate this by just being present at the program as a married couple.

In this chapter there is an emphasis on the personal beliefs and spiritualities of the individual person and couple. The goal of the session is to get the couple to reflect on this and discover that faith element. Most engaged couples are at that stage of faith development in which they are still wrestling with basic questions about their own beliefs. In general, they tend to reject, or at least be apathetic to, religion and its institutions. After several years of marriage, they will mature in their faith. But, generally speaking, at this stage it's enough to get them talking about some of the more primary elements of their spirituality.

Be careful not to evangelize, preach, or "talk down" to the engaged couples. As with the other topics in this book, the team couple is to speak about their own stories. Their presentation on spirituality can present some of the concepts of sacramentality, faith, and religious teachings, but the emphasis should be on the discovery of the couple to the presence of God in their lives.

Finally, the role of Jesus in a couple's married life needs to be addressed. It is obvious, and yet so often overlooked: if the couple is seeking a sacramental marriage in the church, this presupposes some degree of faith in Jesus. You are not to measure the faith readiness of any couple. How could you? Rather, you are to assume, and build on the faith present in each individual. Remember, the most cynical looking couple in your group may in fact be the most faith-filled.

Our Spirituality
Talk Outline

1. Introduce self and topic
- Number of years married?
- Any children? Ages?
- Town you live in? Church?
- How long involved as a marriage preparation volunteer couple?
- Any other general information about yourselves?
- What's your topic?
- Why is it important for them, as engaged couples, to hear about this topic?

2. Marital spirituality. A very broad topic covering a wide spectrum of issues; not just a "church thing."
We'll cover 2 major aspects of your spirituality as a couple: religion and relationship.

3. Spirituality, the relationship that you have with God
- It means recognizing God's presence in your life and developing a relationship with this God through prayer, church participation, or other means.
- It means living in accord with your understanding of God's plan for your life.
- It means becoming one and living out to the fullest, the sacrament that you are.
- It also means accepting your role as steward or caretaker of the earth, animals, and humanity. Here it is your responsibility as a creation of God to feed the hungry, clothe the naked, and shelter the homeless.

4. Religion refers to
- your religious identity (Christian, Jewish, Muslim, etc.).
- the denomination you belong to (Roman Catholic, Lutheran, Episcopalian, Methodist, etc.).
- worship—how, when, where, why and with whom you do it.
- rituals—what, where, when, why, how, and with whom you do them.
- beliefs—what you believe about God, Jesus, the church, etc.

5. Relationship
The quality of your relationships exhibits for yourself and for others the quality of your response to God's presence in your life and to your acceptance of your role as steward. These relationships include:
- your relationship with God.
- your relationship with each other.
- your relationship with a community that shares common experiences, values, worship, and faith.

6. Blending of religion and relationships in a marriage, and especially in an interfaith marriage, needs to be handled in the following ways:

- lovingly—accepting each other unconditionally
- respectfully—valuing each other's opinions, thoughts, and feelings
- with good communication skills—listening and asking appropriate questions
- with trust and openness
- with effort and sincerity in trying to find an agreed upon common ground that both partners can embrace and accept.

NOTES:

1. Read the couple's and leader's edition chapters on this topic.
2. Lace this and all talks with personal stories, examples, and anecdotes that add color and/or demonstrate what you are talking about.

Notes

Our Spirituality

When Mike and Jean announced their engagement, her parents were relieved. Jean had been seriously dating another man who was Protestant. Her parents, devout Catholics, were uncomfortable with the idea of their daughter in a "mixed marriage." They had hoped and prayed that Jean would marry someone like Mike, someone with the same faith. And now their wish had come true.

Unfortunately, Jean's parents actually were not getting what they wanted. Their daughter is indeed marrying another Catholic. But that is no guarantee that Jean and Mike have a similar "faith." Their marriage, like most marriages, will be a "mixed" marriage. Each of them has had a different experience of religion, a different spirituality, and a different perspective of the role of Christ, and God, in their lives. So while both indeed call themselves Catholic, they may mean very different things.

To one degree or another, we are all "interfaith" couples, regardless of whether or not we have been raised in or practice the same faith. We can testify to this in our own marriage. We were each born and raised Roman Catholic, and therefore we share many similar experiences and memories. However, our individual relationships with God are quite different. Each of our approaches to prayer, to Jesus, to church, to the holiness of our surroundings, are marked by subtle and some not so subtle differences. Over the years we have discovered that while we each can continue our individual spiritualities, we are also able to combine the two to form "our" spirituality as a couple. Such diversity within a similar religious tradition is a wonderful thing! It has added tremendously to

75

NOTE: This page is reproduced from the Couple's Book.

INTERFAITH MARRIAGES

Marriages within the church in which a Catholic marries a non-Catholic are commonplace today. A study by the United States Catholic Conference, "Empirical Research on Interfaith Marriages in America," concluded that:

1. Attitudes toward interfaith marriages are becoming more favorable;

2. The rate of interfaith marriages will continue to grow;

3. For every interfaith marriage that remains mixed, there is one in which one spouse converts to the other's religion;

4. Nearly all conversions take place at the time of marriage or before the first child is ten years old;

5. Continued religious differences within a marriage tend to reduce marital satisfaction and decrease church involvement;

6. The mother usually has a stronger influence on the children's religious identification than the father;

7. Disagreement over children's religious upbringing is one of the most common causes of strife in interfaith marriages;

8. Interfaith marriages have a higher percentage of divorce than same-faith marriages.

One point not mentioned on this list is the potential that interfaith marriages have to enrich their church and community. An interfaith couple who possess a loving, nonjudgmental relationship can be a symbol of acceptance and cooperation for all to see.

the vitality of our marriage and to the depths of our individual experiences of God.

Discovering your spirituality as a couple takes time. But like all aspects of your relationship, it will develop and grow. Communicating about your own spirituality honestly and lovingly opens the way to a relationship with God that best reflects who the two of you are as a couple.

The foundation of your marital spirituality is the individual experiences, beliefs, and perceptions that you each bring to your relationship. A good way to start to uncover and identify these is to answer the following question: "In the midst of great joy or sorrow, where do I find God?" That is a thought-provoking question to answer. We suggest you wrestle with it and discuss it with your partner. This will help your partner understand more about your unique relationship with God and will ultimately lead to your new spirituality as a couple.

As with most of the issues affecting your relationship, your relationship with God has been influenced by your family. As we explained in Chapter Four, you are a product of your upbringing. Therefore, your spirituality is a product of the spirituality of your family of origin. This doesn't mean that what you do and what your parents do are identical, but that there are similarities. The family has been called the "domestic church," for out of our family life springs the worshiping practices and faith of every individual. It is within our families that we first experienced love and tenderness, and that we first learned to pray. And it was within our family's life that we first experienced the love of God through our love for each other. Family life is sacred. When most of us reflect back on our family lives, it's hard to believe that anything so ordinary as the daily routine of getting food on the table and raising children could possibly be holy. Yet we believe it is. Jesus' birth into a family was not mere coincidence. It is within the family that the sacred in the ordinary is found, and we rediscover the love of God which unites us all.

Choosing to be married in the Catholic church means that you are accepting the responsibilities of living out a sacramental marriage. And what does that mean? Living a sacramental marriage means that you and your partner make a covenant with God to live a life that reflects to the world the love of God. The Bible compares the love of a wife and a husband to the love that God has for God's people. Your responsibility then is to love each other unconditionally, as God loves us.

76

NOTE: This page is reproduced from the Couple's Book.

Most people believe that the priest marries you. This is not true. The real ministers of your sacrament are the two of you. During the wedding ceremony, when you give your mutual consent, you marry each other. In this way marriage is the unique sacrament among the seven. And it further emphasizes the point that being married in the church is something not to be taken lightly. Ask yourself again why you are about to have a church wedding. Is it because of parental pressure? Or because it will look good? Or because you always dreamed of being married in a church? Or is it because you value your faith and want to live out that faith in a covenant relationship with your partner and God within the context of a worshipping community? By seeking a church wedding you are making a decision to live out a sacramental marriage, which means you are committing yourself to a permanent, exclusive relationship of love and responsibility with your partner.

ROMANCING EARTH

"Recycle, Reuse, Reduce." These are the three Rs of our environmentally conscious society today. As a culture, we are becoming increasingly aware of our responsibility to Mother Earth, and are making collective and individual attempts to become better stewards of our precious planet.

A steward is someone who is responsible for the safety and well-being of that which has been given. A steward oversees that the use of this "given" is prudent, caring, life-giving. A steward realizes that you don't truly own, but rather are just temporarily responsible. God has assigned us to be stewards of our planet.

Our stewardship should dictate that we drop our consumer mentality and adopt a relationship mentality with the land, water, air, and animals. As with your relationship as a young couple in love, our relationship with the environment should be characterized by a healthy give and take, respect and selfless love. The hallmark of a young couple's relationship is romance. Your partner is precious to you; you treat your partner with tenderness. We would do well to model our relationship with Mother Earth on our relationship with one we love, and maintain the romance with Mother Earth.

DIVORCE AND ANNULMENT

Many Catholics today confuse divorce and annulment. Some believe that annulments are simply church divorces. But according to church teaching, there is a very real difference between divorce and annulment. An annulment is an official church declaration that a valid sacramental marriage never existed in the first place. A divorce is a civil declaration that a valid marriage did exist, but it has now been ended.

There are many grounds for a church annulment. Some are: lack of maturity at the time of the wedding; lack of proper form, i.e. the presence of a priest or deacon and two witnesses; moral impotency; failure of being open to having children; prior intention to be unfaithful; psychopathology and/or schizophrenia; psychic incompetence; alcoholism or addiction.

However, the number one ground for annulments is the lack of discretion; in other words, the individual(s) did not understand the nature of living out a sacramental marriage at the time of the wedding.

Annulments are handled through the tribunal of each diocese. The annulment process can take from a few months to a few years and may cost several hundred dollars to complete. Two myths about annulments need to be dispelled: (1) children from an annulled marriage are not considered illegitimate, and (2) civilly divorced Catholics who remarry without an annulment are not automatically excommunicated. For more information, contact the tribunal in your diocese.

NOTE: This page is reproduced from the Couple's Book.

His Page

Answer these questions by yourself. When you are finished share them with your partner.

1. When I was a child, my family of origin: (check all that apply)

    ☐ went to Mass/worship service every Sunday

    ☐ went one or two times a month

    ☐ went a couple of times a year

    ☐ placed a high priority on our faith

    ☐ read the Bible

    ☐ prayed together

    ☐ had little to do with religion, church, or faith

2. How important is my faith to me now? Circle one:

    very important   somewhat important   not important

3. Why am I getting married in the church?

4. Do I know what you think about God? Jesus?

5. How important is it for me to raise our children in my faith?

NOTE: This page is reproduced from the Couple's Book.

6. What religious traditions are most important to me, for example, midnight Mass on Christmas Eve, the Easter Vigil, a big party for a baby's christening?

7. Do I think that God has a place in our marriage? What is it?

8. Is religion a source of conflict for us?

9. When I think about our marriage as a sacrament, I feel

10. I have felt that God has been present in my life, usually when

11. In the midst of great joy or sorrow, where do I find God?

12. If Jesus had one day to spend with us, what would he want to teach us?

80

NOTE: This page is reproduced from the Couple's Book.

Her Page

Answer these questions by yourself. When you are finished share them with your partner.

1. When I was a child, my family of origin: (check all that apply)

    ☐ went to Mass/worship service every Sunday

    ☐ went one or two times a month

    ☐ went a couple of times a year

    ☐ placed a high priority on our faith

    ☐ read the Bible

    ☐ prayed together

    ☐ had little to do with religion, church, or faith

2. How important is my faith to me now? Circle one:

    very important   somewhat important   not important

3. Why am I getting married in the church?

4. Do I know what you think about God? Jesus?

5. How important is it for me to raise our children in my faith?

NOTE: This page is reproduced from the Couple's Book.

6. What religious traditions are most important to me, for example, midnight Mass on Christmas Eve, the Easter Vigil, a big party for a baby's christening?

7. Do I think that God has a place in our marriage? What is it?

8. Is religion a source of conflict for us?

9. When I think about our marriage as a sacrament, I feel

10. I have felt that God has been present in my life, usually when

11. In the midst of great joy or sorrow, where do I find God?

12. If Jesus had one day to spend with us, what would he want to teach us?

NOTE: This page is reproduced from the Couple's Book.

Group Section

1. If Jesus were to return today as a married individual, what kind of relationship would he have with his wife? How would Jesus settle a disagreement with his wife?

2. What is the difference between organized religion and faith?

3. Discuss whether religious traditions and rituals should be an important part of your future marriage and family life.

4. Discuss what it means to be "spiritual." How do you share your spirituality with each other?

Issues of Special Focus

If you lived together before you were married in the church:

1. In what ways do you think that your faith has changed as a result of living with your partner?

2. In what ways has your practice of your religion changed?

3. Do you think marriage will change any of these answers? How? Why?

If one or both of you has a child or children from a previous relationship, please discuss the following:

1. How does having a child affect the practice of religious traditions and customs?

2. Discuss the religious values you would each want children to have. List and discuss the five most important ones.

3. If you disagree, how will you deal with the child's religious upbringing? Who could you discuss this with?

4. If you are from a religious tradition other than Catholic and your partner is Catholic, how can your partner share his/her Catholic faith with the child(ren)? Be creative.

5. What are the family pressures or expectations on how your children should be raised in their faith?

6. What, if any, are the influences of the child's other biological parent on this issue?

If you are a couple with mixed religious faiths:

1. How does the partner who holds religious beliefs other than Catholic feel about having a Catholic church wedding?

2. How do each of you feel about the Catholic partner having to promise to raise the children in the Catholic faith? Will you do it?

3. If one of you is non-Christian, will you observe the religious traditions and holidays of both faiths?

4. Discuss how each of you feels about observing the traditions of the other.

Relationship Check

Each of you should circle the number that best represents how you feel about your relationship after discussing these topics. Remember, you each need to select your own number.

1. very close   2. somewhat close   3. somewhat distant   4. very distant

What do I want to discuss further with you?

NOTE: This page is reproduced from the Couple's Book.

Planning Our Wedding Liturgy

Let's look at two imaginary couples, each with an opposing, extreme attitude toward their wedding liturgies. Couple A could not care less about their wedding ceremony. They are really more into preparing for the wedding reception: who to invite, what band to hire, how to deal with Uncle Henry when he has had too much to drink, and so on. They plan to leave the wedding preparation "stuff" to the priest—the selection of the readings, the responses, the hymns, and even the wording of the wedding vows—since he's the "pro" anyway.

Couple Z wants the perfect wedding liturgy in which everything has a private meaning to them. The songs will be "their songs." The readings will be from their favorite poems. They want everything to symbolize their unique love for each other, and they want to softly whisper their vows to each other since it is the ultimate symbolic expression of their love.

Couple A is apathetic regarding their wedding liturgy and would be happy with a generic, "canned" Mass. Couple Z wants such a personal experience that they really don't need anyone else to be present. Now neither of these extreme couples represent you, of course—or do they?

Between these two extreme cases is a continuum of acceptable ways to approach your wedding liturgy. Here are a few ideas for you to consider.

NUPTIAL MASS?

The first and probably most significant decision you should make is whether you wish to have your wedding ceremony within the Liturgy of the Eucharist or outside of it, with Mass or without Mass. The wedding without a Mass may be the best ceremony for you if, for example, one of you is not Catholic. Both ceremonies would be the same up to and including the Rite of Matrimony. But they differ after that, as you can see from the following outlines.

PERSONAL OR PRIVATE CEREMONY?

It is your wedding liturgy. Get involved! Be active in selecting the music, the responses, the readings and prayers that will be part of the ceremony. But also remember that it is a liturgy, which is public worship. So, although your wedding should be personal and have your distinctive touch, that does not mean that it should also be private; they are not the same thing. Your wedding should be personal and public;

NOTE: This page is reproduced from the Couple's Book.

it should have your personal mark, but it is also the public proclamation of your love and lifelong commitment. The songs, prayers, and readings should have universal meaning so that all present are drawn into the service as participants and not just as observers.

PROCESSION

More and more couples today no longer follow the custom of the father escorting the bride down the aisle to "give her away" to the groom. This custom has its roots in the days when young women were considered to be the property of the father, and thus were handed over to a new "owner," the groom. Even the veil over the bride's face can be traced to the days when marriages were contracted between families, and the groom did not even know what the bride looked like until the wedding day when the veil was lifted. You may want to consider some of the following alternatives for your wedding procession.

Have the bride's attendants and groom's attendants walk down the aisle together, followed by the groom and his parent(s), followed by the bride and her parent(s). Then both sets of parents present their children to each other. A second suggestion that is especially appropriate for couples who are older or who have been living out of their parents' home for some years is for the bride and groom to walk down the aisle together, without their parents accompanying them. Whatever you decide, just be certain that what you do is representative of you and your relationship, rather than because it's the "expected" way of doing it.

READINGS AND READERS

There are typically two Bible readings. The First Reading is usually from the Hebrew Scriptures (Old Testament) and the Second Reading from the Christian Scriptures (New Testament). Later in this section we list all the Scripture readings from which you may select those you wish to be read during your wedding ceremony.

If the readers are to be friends or family members, stress that they are to practice by reading out loud in front of you as well as from a microphone if one is to be used at the church. Choose readers who will read well, project loud enough to be heard, and who will take this honor seriously.

PRAYERS

There are several options from which to choose. And as with most of your wedding liturgy preparations, we recommend that this be done with the help of the priest or liturgist. All your options are

---

WEDDING WITHIN MASS

1. Introductory Rite
   a. Procession
   b. Collect

2. Liturgy of the Word
   a. Old Testament reading
   b. Psalm response
   c. New Testament reading
   d. Gospel verse
   e. Gospel reading
   f. Homily, or sermon

3. Rite of Marriage
   a. Exchange of vows
   b. Blessing of the rings and giving of rings
   c. Universal Prayer

4. Liturgy of the Eucharist
   a. Preparation of the gifts
   b. Eucharistic Prayer
   c. Nuptial blessing
   d. Communion

5. Concluding Rite and Final Blessing

WEDDING OUTSIDE MASS

1. Introductory Rite
   a. Procession
   b. Collect

2. Liturgy of the Word
   a. Old Testament reading
   b. Psalm response
   c. New Testament reading
   d. Gospel verse
   e. Gospel reading
   f. Homily, or sermon

3. Rite of Marriage
   a. Exchange of vows
   b. Blessing of the rings and giving of rings
   c. Universal Prayer

4. Nuptial Blessing

5. Final Blessing

NOTE: This page is reproduced from the Couple's Book.

listed in this section. We recommend that the Lord's Prayer (Our Father), the universal prayer of all Christians, be recited and not sung, because each denomination has its own way of singing this prayer.

WEDDING VOWS

One of the ways that you can make your wedding unique is through the creation of your own vows. While there are commonly used forms, you have the option of writing your own. We suggest that you discuss this with the liturgist or priest to make sure that what you choose to say is compatible with the context of your wedding liturgy. You might also choose to memorize them and say them to each other without the assistance of the priest.

MUSIC

Selecting appropriate music can be a difficult task for non-musicians. The parish music director, liturgist, organist, or the priest will be able to assist you in selecting music that will draw people into the ceremony, as well as be inspirational and meaningful to you and the church community. Since this is a religious ceremony, the music should be suitable for the worship of God. You may have a beautiful song in mind that would be better played at the reception than at the liturgy. There are hundreds of appropriate liturgical hymns and instrumentals from which to choose. If, however, you find that there are some songs that are so meaningful to you that you want them included in the liturgy, consider using them as people are entering the church and being seated. Also, you should consider what types of musical instruments you will need, such as an organ, a piano, a guitar or two, a flute or a harp. In addition, a leader of song or a cantor adds very much to the overall flow of the ceremony.

LITURGY BOOKLET

In a wedding liturgy booklet, you would list the order of the ceremony, including the words to all the prayers, responses, and songs that the congregation is to recite or sing. Such a booklet, distributed by the ushers, would be a guide to the ceremony and en-courage the people to participate in it. In the booklet you may also list the names of the readers, priest(s)/minister(s), musicians, leader of song, attendants, and any personal message you may want to express to all your family and friends. You may also want to include your married names and new address. Remember to include in the booklet any special permission for the use of songs. Some publishers want specific information about their songs listed. The liturgist or music director would be able to assist you with this.

PHOTOS AND VIDEOS

We suggest that you confer with the parish guidelines regarding the taking of photographs and videotaping. Your wedding is primarily a religious ceremony, an act of worship. Professional photographers and videographers are welcome in most churches, but they have a restricted role and place. They should clearly understand where and when they are allowed to take pictures so that they do not detract from the central focus of the liturgy. Also consider whether you will be distracted by these people and their equipment. Will it make you uncomfortable, nervous, or act unnaturally? If so, consider modifying the number of people doing the shooting and focus more on what is central to this ceremony.

WEDDING LITURGY PLANNING SHEETS

Two planning sheets for your wedding liturgy are provided. The draft copy is your working copy on which you should write your ideas, sharing them with the priest and/or parish liturgist, in order to make your final decisions regarding music, readings, prayers, responses, participants' roles, and various other options. The final copy of your wedding liturgy planning sheet is where you should write the final selections for your wedding that both of you have agreed upon. This is the copy you should submit to the priest.

The pages following these two planning sheets list all the prayers, readings, and responses from which you may make your selections. Read each carefully, and then record the number and letter of the selection in the appropriate space on the planning sheet.

NOTE: This page is reproduced from the Couple's Book.

Wedding Liturgy Planning Sheet
(draft copy)

for _____ and _____
           (bride)   *(groom)*

Wedding date and time_____   Church_____

Rehearsal date and time_____   Priest/minister_____

Maid/matron of honor_____   Best man_____

Bride's attendants_____   _____

_____   _____

_____   _____

Groom's attendants_____   _____

_____   _____

_____   _____

Will the wedding be: Within Mass_____?   Outside Mass_____?

Do we plan to have the following?

Organist   ☐ No ☐ Yes _____

Leader of song   ☐ No ☐ Yes _____

Other musicians   ☐ No ☐ Yes _____   _____

Ring bearer   ☐ No ☐ Yes _____

Flower girl   ☐ No ☐ Yes _____

Altar servers   ☐ No ☐ Yes _____   _____

Liturgy booklet   ☐ No ☐ Yes

Unity candle   ☐ No ☐ Yes

Eucharistic ministers   ☐ No ☐ Yes _____

Welcoming music   ☐ No ☐ Yes _____   _____

Musician(s)/singer(s)   ☐ No ☐ Yes _____   _____

Introductory Rite

Processional hymn/music ☐ No ☐ Yes _____

Musician(s)/singer(s)   ☐ No ☐ Yes _____   _____

Collect *(page 91-92)* (circle)   1   2   3   4   5   6

87

NOTE: This page is reproduced from the Couple's Book.

Liturgy of the Word

The Old Testament *(pages 93-96)*   #_____   Reader_____

Responsorial psalm *(pages 97-98)*   #_____   Reader/singer_____

The New Testament *(pages 99-103)*   #_____   Reader_____

Gospel acclamation *(page 104)*   #_____   Reader/singer_____

Gospel *(pages 105-108)*   #_____

Rite of Matrimony

Exchange of wedding vows *(pages 109-110)*: Consent (circle)   1   2   3   4
Reception of Consent   1   2

Blessing and Giving of Rings *(page 111)* (circle)   1   2   3

The *Arras* or the *Lazo* or the Veil *(page 112)*   ☐ No   ☐ Yes _____

Universal Prayer *(indicate special intentions)*   Reader_____

_____   _____

_____   _____

_____   _____

Liturgy of the Eucharist

Gift bearers_____   _____

Presentation hymn_____

Musician(s)/singer(s)_____   _____   _____

Prayer over the offerings *(page 114)* (circle)   1   2   3

Preface *(page 115)* (circle)   1   2   3

Nuptial blessing *(pages 116-118)*

Introduction (circle)   1   2   3   4

Blessing (circle)   1   2   3

Communion hymn_____

Meditation hymn_____

Musician(s)/singer(s)_____

Prayer after communion *(page 119)* (circle)   1   2   3

Concluding Rite

Final blessing *(page 120)* (circle)   1   2   3

Recessional hymn_____

Musician(s)/singer(s)_____   _____   _____

Questions we need to ask, and things we need to do:

88

NOTE: This page is reproduced from the Couple's Book.

Wedding Liturgy Planning Sheet

(final copy)

for _____ and _____
       (bride)   *(groom)*

Wedding date and time_____   Church_____

Rehearsal date and time_____   Priest/minister_____

Maid/matron of honor_____   Best man_____

Bride's attendants_____   _____

_____   _____

_____   _____

Groom's attendants_____   _____

_____   _____

_____   _____

Will the wedding be: Within Mass_____?   Outside Mass_____?

Do we plan to have the following?

Organist	☐ No	☐ Yes	_____	
Leader of song	☐ No	☐ Yes	_____	
Other musicians	☐ No	☐ Yes	_____	_____
Ring bearer	☐ No	☐ Yes	_____	
Flower girl	☐ No	☐ Yes	_____	
Altar servers	☐ No	☐ Yes	_____	_____
Liturgy booklet	☐ No	☐ Yes		
Unity candle	☐ No	☐ Yes		
Eucharistic ministers	☐ No	☐ Yes	_____	_____
Welcoming music	☐ No	☐ Yes	_____	_____
Musician(s)/singer(s)	☐ No	☐ Yes	_____	_____

Introductory Rite

Processional hymn/music	☐ No	☐ Yes	_____	
Musician(s)/singer(s)	☐ No	☐ Yes	_____	_____
Collect *(page 91-92)* (circle)		1 2 3 4 5 6		

89

NOTE: This page is reproduced from the Couple's Book.

Liturgy of the Word

The Old Testament *(pages 93-96)*	#_____	Reader_____
Responsorial psalm *(pages 97-98)*	#_____	Reader/singer_____
The New Testament *(pages 99-103)*	#_____	Reader_____
Gospel acclamation *(page 104)*	#_____	Reader/singer_____
Gospel *(pages 105-108)*	#_____	

Rite of Matrimony

Exchange of wedding vows *(pages 109-110)*: Consent (circle)   1   2   3   4
Reception of Consent   1   2

Blessing and Giving of Rings *(page 111)* (circle)   1   2   3

The *Arras* or the *Lazo* or the Veil *(page 112)*   ☐ No   ☐ Yes _____

Universal Prayer *(indicate special intentions)*   Reader_____

_____   _____

_____   _____

_____   _____

Liturgy of the Eucharist

Gift bearers_____   _____

Presentation hymn_____

Musician(s)/singer(s)_____   _____   _____

Prayer over the offerings *(page 114)* (circle)   1   2   3

Preface *(page 115)* (circle)   1   2   3

Nuptial blessing *(pages 116-118)*

Introduction (circle)   1   2   3   4

Blessing (circle)   1   2   3

Communion hymn_____

Meditation hymn_____

Musician(s)/singer(s)_____

Prayer after communion *(page 119)* (circle)   1   2   3

Concluding Rite

Final blessing *(page 120)* (circle)   1   2   3

Recessional hymn_____

Musician(s)/singer(s)_____   _____   _____

Questions we need to ask, and things we need to do:

90

NOTE: This page is reproduced from the Couple's Book.

The Marriage Liturgy

Here is the basic outline of the wedding liturgy. But there are differences in the rite, depending on whether the wedding is celebrated within Mass, without Mass, or when a Catholic is marrying a Catechumen or an unbaptized person. There are also a few adjustments made when the couple is past childbearing age. Be sure to talk to the ministers who are helping you prepare. They will guide you through these details.

COLLECT

The Collect (the opening prayer) sets the tone for the rest of your wedding liturgy. You will find the selections available listed below. Read through each and select the one that you would like to have the priest and/or minister pray to begin your wedding liturgy. (If you choose the first nuptial blessing on page 116, then do not choose the first Collect shown below.)

OPTION 1
O God, who consecrated the bond of Marriage
by so great a mystery
that in the wedding covenant you foreshadow
the Sacrament of Christ and his Church,
grant, we pray, to these your servants,
that what they receive in faith
they may live out in deeds.
Through our Lord Jesus Christ, your Son,
who lives and reigns with you in the unity
    of the Holy Spirit,
one God, for ever and ever.

OPTION 2
O God, who in creating the human race
willed that man and wife should be one,
join, we pray, in a bond of inseparable love
these your servants who are to be united
    in the covenant of Marriage,
so that, as you make their love fruitful,
they may become, by your grace,
    witnesses to charity itself.
Through our Lord Jesus Christ, your Son,
who lives and reigns with you in the unity
    of the Holy Spirit,
one God, for ever and ever.

OPTION 3
Be attentive to our prayers, O Lord,
and in your kindness
pour out your grace on these your servants
    (N. and N.),
that, coming together before your altar,
they may be confirmed in love for one another.
Through our Lord Jesus Christ, your Son,
who lives and reigns with you in the unity
    of the Holy Spirit,
one God, for ever and ever.

OPTION 4
Grant, we pray, almighty God,
that these your servants,
now to be joined by the Sacrament of Matrimony,
may grow in the faith they profess
and enrich your Church with faithful offspring.
Through our Lord Jesus Christ, your Son,
who lives and reigns with you in the unity
    of the Holy Spirit,
one God, for ever and ever.

91

NOTE: This page is reproduced from the Couple's Book.

OPTION 5

Be attentive to our prayers, O Lord,
and in your kindness uphold
what you have established for the increase
   of the human race,
so that the union you have created
may be kept safe by your assistance.
Through our Lord Jesus Christ, your Son,
who lives and reigns with you in the unity
   of the Holy Spirit,
one God, for ever and ever.

OPTION 6

O God, who since the beginning of the world
have blessed the increase of offspring,
show favor to our supplications
and pour forth the help of your blessing
on these your servants (N. and N.),
so that in the union of Marriage
they may be bound together
in mutual affection,
in likeness of mind,
and in shared holiness.
Through our Lord Jesus Christ, your Son,
who lives and reigns with you in the unity
   of the Holy Spirit,
one God, for ever and ever.

92

NOTE: This page is reproduced from the Couple's Book.

Liturgy of the Word

The readings given here, pages 93–108, are the readings that can be used in your wedding liturgy. The Order of Celebrating Matrimony states that "at least one reading that explicitly speaks of Marriage must always be chosen." These readings are designated here by an asterisk.

READING FROM THE OLD TESTAMENT

The first reading is typically taken from the Old Testament. (If you are getting married during the Easter season, however, then your first reading should be Revelation 19: 1, 5–9a, shown in this book in the New Testament readings, number 14 on page 103.)

Throughout the Old Testament we read of God's great love for God's people, first in the book of Genesis, in the creation stories, and continuing on in stories of the love between a man and a woman. Each of the selections here has its own message, its own theme. Read them carefully. Once you have made your selection, think too about who you would like to have read this. Would they read it well and convey its message? Once you have decided, list your choice at the appropriate place on your planning sheet.

OPTION 1

A reading from the Book of Genesis *(1:26–28, 31a)**

Then God said:
"Let us make man in our image, after our likeness.
Let them have dominion over the fish of the sea,
   the birds of the air, and the cattle,
   and over all the wild animals
   and all the creatures that crawl on the ground.

God created man in his image;
   in the image of God he created him;
   male and female he created them.

God blessed them, saying:
   "Be fertile and multiply;
   fill the earth and subdue it.
Have dominion over the fish of the sea,
   the birds of the air;
   and all the living things that move on the earth."
God looked at everything he had made,
   and he found it very good.

OPTION 2

A reading from the Book of Genesis *(2:18–24)**

The Lord God said: "It is not good for the man
      to be alone.
I will make a suitable partner for him."
So the Lord God formed out of the ground
      various wild animals and various birds of the air,
      and he brought them to the man to see what
      he would call them;
      whatever the man called each of them
         would be its name.
The man gave names to all the cattle,
      all the birds of the air, and all wild animals;
      but none proved to be the suitable partner
         for the man.

So the Lord God cast a deep sleep on the man,
      and while he was asleep,
      he took out one of his ribs and closed up its
         place with flesh.
The Lord God then built up into a woman the rib
      that he had taken from the man.
When he brought her to the man, the man said:

   "This one, at last, is bone of my bones
      and flesh of my flesh;

93

NOTE: This page is reproduced from the Couple's Book.

This one shall be called 'woman,'
    for out of 'her man' this one has been taken."

That is why a man leaves his father and mother
    and clings to his wife,
    and the two of them become one body.

OPTION 3
A reading from the Book of Genesis *(24:48–51, 58–67)**

The servant of Abraham said to Laban:
"I bowed down in worship to the LORD,
    blessing the LORD, the God of my master Abraham,
    who had led me on the right road
    to obtain the daughter of my master's kinsman
      for his son.
If, therefore, you have in mind to show true
      loyalty to my master,
    let me know;
    but if not, let me know that, too.
I can then proceed accordingly."

Laban and his household said in reply:
    "This thing comes from the LORD;
    we can say nothing to you either for or against it.
Here is Rebekah, ready for you;
    take her with you,
    that she may become the wife
      of your master's son,
    as the LORD has said."

So they called Rebekah and asked her,
    "Do you wish to go with this man?"
She answered, "I do."
At this they allowed their sister Rebekah
      and her nurse to take leave,
    along with Abraham's servant and his men.
Invoking a blessing on Rebekah, they said:

    "Sister, may you grow
      into thousands of myriads;
    And may your descendants gain possession
      of the gates of their enemies!"

Then Rebekah and her maids started out;
    they mounted their camels and followed the man.
So the servant took Rebekah and went on his way.

Meanwhile Isaac had gone from Beer-lahai-roi
    and was living in the region of the Negeb.

_____
94

One day toward evening he went out…
    in the field,
    and as he looked around, he noticed
      that camels were approaching.
Rebekah, too, was looking about, and when she saw him,
    she alighted from her camel and asked the servant,
    "Who is the man out there, walking through
      the fields toward us?"
"That is my master," replied the servant.
Then she covered herself with her veil.

The servant recounted to Isaac all the things he had done.
Then Isaac took Rebekah into his tent;
    he married her, and thus she became his wife.
In his love for her Isaac found solace
    after the death of his mother Sarah.

OPTION 4
A reading from the Book of Tobit *(7:6–14)**

Raphael and Tobiah entered the house of Raguel
    and greeted him.
Raguel sprang up and kissed Tobiah,
    shedding tears of joy.
But when he heard that Tobit had lost his eyesight,
    he was grieved and wept aloud.
He said to Tobiah:
    "My child, God bless you!
You are the son of a noble and good father.
But what a terrible misfortune
    that such a righteous and charitable man
    should be afflicted with blindness!"
He continued to weep in the arms of his
      kinsman Tobiah.
His wife Edna also wept for Tobit;
    and even their daughter Sarah began to weep.

Afterward, Raguel slaughtered a ram from the flock
    and gave them a cordial reception.
When they had bathed and reclined to eat,
    Tobiah said to Raphael, "Brother Azariah,
    ask Raguel to let me marry my
      kinswoman Sarah."
Raguel overheard the words;
    so he said to the boy:
    "Eat and drink and be merry tonight,
    for no man is more entitled to marry my
      daughter Sarah

NOTE: This page is reproduced from the Couple's Book.

than you, brother.
Besides, not even I have the right to give her
    to anyone but you,
        because you are my closest relative.
But I will explain the situation to you very frankly.
I have given her in marriage to seven men,
    all of whom were kinsman of ours,
    and all died on the very night
        they approached her.
But now, son, eat and drink.
I am sure the Lord will look after you both."
Tobiah answered, "I will eat or drink nothing
    until you set aside what belongs to me."

Raguel said to him: "I will do it.
She is yours according to the decree
    of the Book of Moses.
Your marriage to her has been decided in heaven!
Take your kinswoman
    from now on you are her love,
    and she is your beloved.
She is yours today and ever after.
And tonight, son, may the Lord of heaven
        prosper you both.
May he grant you mercy and peace."
Then Raguel called his daughter Sarah,
    and she came to him.
He took her by the hand and gave her to Tobiah
    with the words:
    "Take her according to the law.
According to the decree written in the
    Book of Moses she is your wife.
Take her and bring her back safely to your father.
And may the God of heaven grant both of you
        peace and prosperity."
He then called her mother and told her
    to bring a scroll,
        so that he might draw up a marriage contract
        stating that he gave Sarah to Tobiah as his wife
        according to the decree of the Mosaic law.
Her mother brought the scroll,
    and he drew up the contract,
    to which they affixed their seal.

Afterward they began to eat and drink.

OPTION 5

A reading from the Book of Tobit *(8:4b–9)**

On their wedding night Tobiah arose from bed
    and said to his wife,
    "Sister, get up. Let us pray and beg our Lord
    to have mercy on us and to grant us
        deliverance."
Sarah got up, and they started to pray
    and beg that deliverance might be theirs.
They began with these words:

    "Blessed are you, O God of our fathers;
        praised be your name forever and ever.
    Let the heavens and all your creation
        praise you forever.
    You made Adam and you gave him his wife Eve
        to be his help and support;
        and from these two the human race descended.
    You said, 'It is not good for the man to be alone;
        let us make him a partner like himself.'
    Now, Lord, you know that I take this wife of mine
        not because of lust,
        but for a noble purpose.
    Call down your mercy on me and on her,
        and allow us to live together to a happy old age."

They said together, "Amen, amen."

OPTION 6

A reading from the Book of Proverbs
(31:10–13, 19–20, 30–31)*

When one finds a worthy wife,
    her value is far beyond pearls.
Her husband, entrusting his heart to her,
    has an unfailing prize.
She brings him good, and not evil,
    all the days of her life.
She obtains wool and flax
    and makes cloth with skillful hands.
She puts her hands to the distaff,
    and her fingers ply the spindle.
She reaches out her hands to the poor,
    and extends her arms to the needy.
Charm is deceptive and beauty fleeting;
    the woman who fears the LORD is to be praised.
Give her a reward of her labors,
    and let her works praise her at the city gates.

———
95

NOTE: *This page is reproduced from the Couple's Book.*

A reading from the Song of Songs
(2:8–10, 14, 16a; 8:6–7a)

Hark! my lover—here he comes
    springing across the mountains,
    leaping across the hills.
My lover is like a gazelle
    or a young stag.
Here he stands behind our wall,
    gazing through the windows,
    peering through the lattices.
My lover speaks; he says to me,
    "Arise, my beloved, my dove, my beautiful one,
      and come!

"O my dove in the clefts of the rock,
    in the secret recesses of the cliff,
Let me see you,
    let me hear your voice,
For your voice is sweet,
    and you are lovely."

My lover belongs to me and I to him.
    He says to me:

"Set me as a seal on your heart,
    as a seal on your arm;
For stern as death is love,
    relentless as the nether world is devotion;
    its flames are a blazing fire.
Deep waters cannot quench love,
    nor floods sweep it away."

A reading from the Book of Sirach *(26:1–4, 13–16)**

Blessed the husband of a good wife;
    twice-lengthened are his days;
A worthy wife brings joy to her husband,
    peaceful and full is his life.
A good wife is a generous gift
    bestowed upon him who fears the LORD;
Be he rich or poor, his heart is content,
    and a smile is ever on his face.

A gracious wife delights her husband,
    her thoughtfulness puts flesh on his bones;
A gift from the LORD is her governed speech,
    and her firm virtue is of surpassing worth.

Choicest of blessings is a modest wife,
    priceless her chaste soul.
A holy and decent woman adds grace upon grace;
    indeed, no price is worthy of her
      temperate soul.
Like the sun rising in the LORD's heavens,
    the beauty of a virtuous wife is the radiance
      of her home.

A reading from the Book of the Prophet Jeremiah
(31:31–32a, 33–34a)

The days are coming, says the LORD,
    when I will make a new covenant with the
      house of Israel
    and the house of Judah.
It will not be like the covenant I made
    with their fathers:
    the day I took them by the hand
    to lead them forth from the land of Egypt.
But this is the covenant which I will make
    with the house of Israel after those days,
      says the LORD.
I will place my law within them, and write it
    upon their hearts;
    I will be their God, and they shall be my people.
No longer will they have need to teach their
    friends and relatives
    how to know the LORD.
All, from least to greatest, shall know me,
    says the LORD.

NOTE: This page is reproduced from the Couple's Book.

RESPONSORIAL PSALM

In addition to the psalm (or part of psalm) you choose to include in your wedding liturgy, you also have to decide whether to have it read or sung. There are beautiful musical arrangements for some of these psalms and they can enrich your ceremony. Discuss this with your leader of song or parish music director and listen to some of the options. If you do choose to have it sung, remember to include the words in your liturgy booklet if you want the community to sing it. If you choose to have it read, think carefully about the reader. Psalms were written as poems or songs. Will your reader be able to read it that way? List your choice on your planning sheet along with the name of the reader or soloist.

OPTION 1
Psalm 33:12 and 18, 20–21, 22

℟. *The earth is full of the goodness of the Lord.*

Blessed the nation whose God is the Lᴏʀᴅ,
  the people he has chosen as his heritage.
Yes, the Lᴏʀᴅ's eyes are on those who fear him,
  who hope in his merciful love. ℟.

Our soul is waiting for the Lᴏʀᴅ.
  He is our help and our shield.
In him do our hearts find joy.
  We trust in his holy name. ℟.

May your merciful love be upon us,
  as we hope in you, O Lᴏʀᴅ. ℟.

OPTION 2
Psalm 34:2–3, 4–5, 6–7, 8–9

℟. *I will bless the Lord at all times.*
Or: ℟. *Taste and see the goodness of the Lord.*

I will bless the Lᴏʀᴅ at all times,
  praise of him is always in my mouth.
In the Lᴏʀᴅ my soul shall make its boast;
  the humble shall hear and be glad. ℟.

Glorify the Lᴏʀᴅ with me;
  together let us praise his name.
I sought the Lᴏʀᴅ, and he answered me;
  from all my terrors he set me free. ℟.

Look toward him and be radiant;
  let your faces not be abashed.
This lowly one called; the Lᴏʀᴅ heard,
  and rescued him from all his distress. ℟.

The angel of the Lᴏʀᴅ is encamped
  around those who fear him, to rescue them.
Taste and see that the Lᴏʀᴅ is good.
  Blessed the man who seeks refuge in him. ℟.

OPTION 3
Psalm 103:1–2, 8 and 13, 17–18a

℟. *The Lord is kind and merciful.*
Or: ℟. *The Lord's kindness is everlasting to those who fear him.*

Bless the Lᴏʀᴅ, O my soul,
  and all within me, his holy name.
Bless the Lᴏʀᴅ, O my soul,
  and never forget all his benefits. ℟.

The Lᴏʀᴅ is compassionate and gracious,
  slow to anger and rich in mercy.
As a father has compassion on his children,
  the Lᴏʀᴅ's compassion is on those who fear him. ℟.

But the mercy of the Lᴏʀᴅ is everlasting
  upon those who hold him in fear,
upon children's children his righteousness,
  for those who keep his covenant. ℟.

OPTION 4
Psalm 112:1bc–2, 3–4, 5–7a, 7b–8, 9

℟. *Blessed the man who greatly delights
in the Lord's commands.*
Or: ℟. *Alleluia.*

Blessed the man who fears the Lᴏʀᴅ,
  who takes great delight in his commandments.
His descendants shall be powerful on earth;
  the generation of the upright will be blest. ℟.

97

NOTE: This page is reproduced from the Couple's Book.

Riches and wealth are in his house;
    his righteousness stands firm forever.
A light rises in the darkness for the upright;
    he is generous, merciful, and righteous. R.

It goes well for the man who deals generously and lends,
    who conducts his affairs with justice.
He will never be moved;
    forever shall the righteous be remembered.
He has no fear of evil news. R.

With a firm heart, he trusts in the Lord.
With a steadfast heart he will not fear;
    he will see the downfall of his foes. R.

Openhanded, he gives to the poor;
    his righteousness stands firm forever.
        His might shall be exalted in glory. R.

OPTION 5
Psalm 128:1–2, 3, 4–5

R. Blessed are those who fear the Lord.
Or: R. See how the Lord blesses those who fear him.

Blessed are all who fear the LORD,
    and walk in his ways!
By the labor of your hands you shall eat.
    You will be blessed and prosper. R.

Your wife like a fruitful vine
    in the heart of your house;
your children like shoots of the olive
    around your table. R.

Indeed thus shall be blessed
    the man who fears the LORD.
May the LORD bless you from Zion
    all the days of your life!
        May you see your children's children. R.

OPTION 6
Psalm 145:8–9, 10 and 15, 17–18

R. How good is the Lord to all.

The LORD is kind and full of compassion,
    slow to anger, abounding in mercy.

How good is the LORD to all,
    compassionate to all his creatures. R.

All your works shall thank you, O LORD,
    and all your faithful ones bless you.
The eyes of all look to you,
    and you give them their food in due season. R.

The LORD is righteous in all his ways,
    and holy in all his deeds.
The LORD is close to all who call him,
    who call on him in truth. R.

OPTION 7
Psalm 148:1–2, 3–4, 9–10, 11–13a, 13c–14a

R. Let all praise the name of the Lord.
Or: R. Alleluia.

Praise the LORD from the heavens;
    praise him in the heights.
Praise him, all his angels;
    praise him, all his hosts. R.

Praise him, sun and moon;
    praise him, all shining stars.
Praise him, highest heavens,
    and the waters above the heavens. R.

Mountains and all hills,
    fruit trees and all cedars,
beasts, both wild and tame,
    creeping things and birds on the wing. R.

Kings of the earth and all peoples,
    princes and all judges of the earth,
young men and maidens as well,
    the old and the young together.
Let them praise the name of the Lord,
    for his name alone is exalted. R.

His splendor above heaven and earth.
    He exalts the strength of his people. R.

NOTE: This page is reproduced from the Couple's Book.

READING FROM THE NEW TESTAMENT

The following selections each have a specific theme. Select a reading that best fits what you want to say about your relationship with each other and with God, and again, be certain that it fits in with the theme of your liturgy. Record your selections and your reader(s) on your planning sheet.

OPTION 1
A reading from the Letter of St. Paul to the Romans *(8:31b–35, 37–39)*

Brothers and sisters:
If God is for us, who can be against us?
He did not spare his own Son
    but handed him over for us all,
    will he not also give us everything else
        along with him?
Who will bring a charge against God's chosen ones?
It is God who acquits us.
Who will condemn?
It is Christ Jesus who died, rather, was raised,
    who also is at the right hand of God,
    who indeed intercedes for us.
What will separate us from the love of Christ?
Will anguish, or distress, or persecution, or famine,
    or nakedness, or peril, or the sword?
No, in all these things, we conquer overwhelmingly
    through him who loved us.
For I am convinced that neither death, nor life,
    nor angels, nor principalities,
    nor present things, not future things,
    nor powers, nor height, nor depth,
    nor any other creature will be able to separate us
    from the love of God in Christ Jesus our Lord.

OPTION 2 *[long form]*
A reading from the Letter of St. Paul to the Romans *(12:1–2, 9–18)*

I urge you, brothers and sisters, by the mercies of God,
    to offer your bodies as a living sacrifice,
    holy and pleasing to God, your spiritual worship.
Do not conform yourselves to this age
    but be transformed by the renewal of your mind,
    that you may discern what is the will of God,
    what is good and pleasing and perfect.

Let love be sincere;

hate what is evil,
    hold on to what is good;
    love one another with mutual affection;
    anticipate one another in showing honor.
Do not grow slack in zeal,
    be fervent in spirit,
    serve the Lord.
Rejoice in hope,
    endure in affliction,
    persevere in prayer.
Contribute to the needs of the holy ones,
    exercise hospitality.
Bless those who persecute you,
    bless and do not curse them.
Rejoice with those who rejoice,
    weep with those who weep.
Have the same regard for one another;
    do not be haughty but associate with the lowly;
    do not be wise in your own estimation.
Do not repay anyone evil for evil;
    be concerned for what is noble in the sight of all.
If possible, on your part, live at peace with all.

OPTION 2 *[short form]*
A reading from the Letter of St. Paul to the Romans *(12:1–2, 9–13)*

I urge you, brothers and sisters, by the mercies
        of God,
    to offer your bodies as a living sacrifice,
    holy and pleasing to God, your spiritual worship.
Do not conform yourselves to this age
    but be transformed by the renewal of your mind,
    that you may discern what is the will of God,
    what is good and pleasing and perfect.

Let love be sincere;
    hate what is evil,
    hold on to what is good;
    love one another with mutual affection;

99

NOTE: This page is reproduced from the Couple's Book.

anticipate one another in showing honor.
Do not glow slack in zeal,
    be fervent in spirit,
    serve the Lord.
Rejoice in hope,
    endure in affliction,
    persevere in prayer.
Contribute to the needs of the holy ones,
    exercise hospitality.

OPTION 3

A reading from the Letter of St. Paul to the Romans *(15:1b–3a, 5–7, 13)*

Brothers and sisters:
We ought to put up with the failings of the weak
    and not to please ourselves;
    let each of us please our neighbor for the good,
    for building up.
For Christ did not please himself.
May the God of endurance and encouragement
    grant you to think in harmony with one another,
    in keeping with Christ Jesus,
    that with one accord you may with one voice
    glorify the God and Father of our Lord Jesus Christ.

Welcome one another, then, as Christ welcomed you,
    for the glory of God.
May the God of hope fill you with all joy
    and peace in believing,
    so that you may abound in hope by the power
    of the Holy Spirit.

OPTION4

A reading from the First Letter of St. Paul to the Corinthians *(6:13c–15a, 17–20)*

Brothers and sisters:
The body is not for immorality, but for the Lord,
    and the Lord is for the body;
    God raised the Lord and will also raise us
    by his power.

Do you not know that your bodies are members
    of Christ?
Whoever is joined to the Lord becomes one
    spirit with him.
Avoid immorality.
Every other sin a person commits is outside
the body,
    but the immoral person sins against his own body.
Do you not know that your body
    is a temple of the Holy Spirit within you,
    whom you have from God, and that you are
        not your own?
For you have been purchased at a price.
Therefore glorify God in your body.

OPTION 5

A reading from the First Letter of St. Paul to the Corinthians *(12:31—13:8a)*

Brothers and sisters:
Strive eagerly for the greatest spiritual gifts.

But I shall show you a still more excellent way.

If I speak in human and angelic tongues
    but do not have love,
    I am a resounding gong or a clashing cymbal.
And if I have the gift of prophecy
    and comprehend all mysteries and all
        knowledge;
    if I have all faith so as to move mountains,
    but do not have love, I am nothing.
If I give away everything I own,
    and if I hand my body over so that I may boast
    but do not have love, I gain nothing.

Love is patient, love is kind.
It is not jealous, is not pompous,
    it is not inflated, it is not rude,
    it does not seek its own interests,
    it is not quick-tempered, it does not brood over
        injury, it does not rejoice over wrongdoing
    but rejoices with the truth.
It bears all things, believes all things,
    hopes all things, endures all things.
Love never fails.

OPTION 6

A reading from the Letter of St. Paul to the Ephesians *(4:1–6)*

Brothers and sisters:
I, a prisoner for the Lord,
    urge you to live in a manner worthy of the call
        you have received,
    with all humility and gentleness, with patience,

100

NOTE: This page is reproduced from the Couple's Book.

bearing with one another through love,
striving to preserve the unity of the Spirit
through the bond of peace: one Body
   and one Spirit,
as you were also called to the one hope
   of your call;
one Lord, one faith, one baptism;
one God and Father of all,
who is over all and through all and in all.

OPTION 7 *[long form]*
A reading from the Letter of St. Paul to the Ephesians *(5:2a 21–33)*

Brothers and sisters:
Live in love, as Christ loved us
   and handed himself over for us.

Be subordinate to one another out of reverence for Christ.
Wives should be subordinate to their husbands
   as to the Lord.
For the husband is head of his wife
   just as Christ is head of the Church,
   he himself the savior of the body.
As the Church is subordinate to Christ,
   so wives should be subordinate
      to their husbands in everything.
Husbands, love your wives,
   even as Christ loved the Church
   and handed himself over for her to sanctify her,
   cleansing her by the bath of water with the word,
   that he might present to himself the Church
      in splendor,
   without spot or wrinkle or any such thing,
   that she might be holy and without blemish.
So also husbands should love their wives
   as their own bodies.
He who loves his wife loves himself.
For no one hates his own flesh
   but rather nourishes and cherishes it,
   even as Christ does the Church,
   because we are members of his Body.

   For this reason a man shall leave his father
      and his mother
      and be joined to his wife,
   and the two shall become one flesh.

This is a great mystery,
   but I speak in reference to Christ and the Church.
In any case, each one of you should love his wife
      as himself,
   and the wife should respect her husband.

OPTION 7 *[short form]*
A reading from the Letter of St. Paul to the Ephesians *(5:2a, 25–32)*

Brothers and sisters:
Live in love, as Christ loved us
   and handed himself over for us.

Husbands, love your wives,
   even as Christ loved the Church
   and handed himself over for her to sanctify her,
   cleansing her by the bath of water with the word,
   that he might present to himself the Church
      in splendor,
   without spot or wrinkle or any such thing,
   that she might be holy and without blemish.
So also husbands should love their wives
   as their own bodies.
He who loves his wife loves himself.
For no one hates his own flesh
   but rather nourishes and cherishes it,
   even as Christ does the Church,
   because we are members of his Body.

   For this reason a man shall leave his father
      and his mother
      and be joined to his wife,
   and the two shall become one flesh.

This is a great mystery,
   but I speak in reference to Christ
      and the Church.

OPTION 8
A reading from the Letter of St. Paul to the Philippians *(4:4–9)*

Brothers and sisters:
Rejoice in the Lord always.
I shall say it again: Rejoice!
Your kindness should be known to all.
The Lord is near.
Have no anxiety at all, but in everything,
   by prayer and petition, with thanksgiving,

NOTE: This page is reproduced from the Couple's Book.

make your requests known to God.
Then the peace of God that surpasses
        all understanding
    will guard your hearts and minds in Christ Jesus.

Finally, brothers and sisters,
    whatever is true, whatever is honorable,
    whatever is just, whatever is pure,
    whatever is lovely, whatever is gracious,
    if there is any excellence
    and if there is anything worthy of praise,
    think about these things.
Keep on doing what you have learned and received
    and heard and seen in me.
Then the God of peace will be with you.

OPTION 9
A reading from the letter
of st. Paul to the Colossians *(3:12–17)*

Brothers and sisters:
Put on, as God's chosen ones, holy and beloved,
    heartfelt compassion, kindness, humility,
        gentleness, and patience,
    bearing with one another and forgiving one another,
    if one has a grievance against another;
    as the Lord has forgiven you, so must you also do.
And over all these put on love,
    that is, the bond of perfection.
And let the peace of Christ control your hearts,
    the peace into which you were also called
        in one Body.
And be thankful.
Let the word of Christ dwell in you richly,
    as in all wisdom you teach and admonish one another,
    singing psalms, hymns, and spiritual songs
    with gratitude in your hearts to God.
And whatever you do, in word or in deed,
    do everything in the name of the Lord Jesus,
    giving thanks to God the Father through him.

OPTION 10
A reading from the Letter
to the Hebrews *(13:1–4a, 5–6b)*

Brothers and sisters:
Let mutual love continue.
Do not neglect hospitality,

for through it some have unknowingly
        entertained angels.
Be mindful of prisoners as if sharing
        their imprisonment,
    and of the ill-treated as of yourselves,
    for you also are in the body.
Let marriage be honored among all
    and the marriage bed be kept undefiled.
Let your life be free from love of money
    but be content with what you have,
    for he has said, *I will never forsake you*
        or abandon you.
Thus we may say with confidence:

> *The Lord is my helper,*
> *and I will not be afraid.*

OPTION 11
A reading from the First Letter of St. Peter *(3:1–9)*

Beloved:
You wives should be subordinate to your husbands so that,
    even if some disobey the word,
    they may be won over without a word by their
        wives' conduct
    when they observe your reverent and chaste behavior.
Your adornment should not be an external one:
    braiding the hair, wearing gold jewelry,
        or dressing in fine clothes,
    but rather the hidden character of the heart,
    expressed in the imperishable beauty
    of a gentle and calm disposition,
    which is precious in the sight of God.
For this is also how the holy women
        who hoped in God
    once used to adorn themselves
    and were subordinate to their husbands;
    thus Sarah obeyed Abraham, calling him "lord."
You are her children when you do what is good
    and fear no intimidation.

Likewise, you husbands should live with your
        wives in understanding,
    showing honor to the weaker female sex,
    since we are joint heirs of the gift of life,
    so that your prayers may not be hindered.

Finally, all of you, be of one mind, sympathetic,
    loving toward one another, compassionate,
        humble.

NOTE: This page is reproduced from the Couple's Book.

Do not return evil for evil, or insult for insult;
  but, on the contrary, a blessing, because to this
    you were called,
  that you might inherit a blessing.

OPTION 12
A reading from the First Letter of St. John *(3:18–24)*

Children, let us love not in word or speech
  but in deed and truth.

Now this is how we shall know that we belong
    to the truth
  and reassure our hearts before him
  in whatever our hearts condemn,
  for God is greater than our hearts and knows
    everything.
Beloved, if our hearts do not condemn us,
  we have confidence in God
  and receive from him whatever we ask,
  because we keep his commandments and do
    what pleases him.
And his commandment is this:
  we should believe in the name of his Son,
    Jesus Christ,
  and love one another just as he commanded us.
Those who keep his commandment remain
    in him, and he in them,
  and the way we know that he remains in us
  is from the Spirit that he gave us.

OPTION 13
A reading from the First Letter of St. John *(4:7–12)*

Beloved, let us love one another,
  because love is of God;
    everyone who loves is begotten by God
      and knows God.
Whoever is without love does not know God,
  for God is love.
In this way the love of God was revealed to us:
  God sent his only-begotten Son into the world
  so that we might have life through him.
In this is love:
  not that we have loved God, but that he loved us
  and sent his Son as expiation for our sins.
Beloved, if God so loved us,
  we also must love one another.

No one has ever seen God.
Yet, if we love one another, God remains in us,
  and his love is brought to perfection in us.

OPTION 14
A reading from the Book of Revelation *(19:1, 5–9a)*

I, John, heard what sounded like the loud voice
  of a great multitude in heaven, saying:

  "Alleluia!
  Salvation, glory, and might belong to our God."

A voice coming from the throne said:

  "Praise our God, all you his servants,
    and you who revere him, small and great."

Then I heard something like the sound
    of a great multitude
  or the sound of rushing water or mighty peals
    of thunder,
  as they said:
    "Alleluia!
  The Lord has established his reign,
    our God, the almighty.
  Let us rejoice and be glad
    and give him glory.
  For the wedding day of the Lamb has come,
    his bride has made herself ready.
  She was allowed to wear
  a bright, clean linen garment."
(The linen represents the righteous deeds of the
    holy ones.)

Then the angel said to me,
  "Write this:
  Blessed are those who have been called
  to the wedding feast of the Lamb."

103

NOTE: This page is reproduced from the Couple's Book.

GOSPEL ACCLAMATION

With your readings selected, you now need to choose an introduction to the good news of Jesus. The Gospel acclamation announces that there is an important reading coming up. When reviewing the acclamations, therefore, select one that truly proclaims what is coming. Ask yourselves which of the following choices appropriately announces the Gospel and emphasizes what is important in our lives as a loving Christian couple?

The reader(s) of the second reading or the leader of song are usually the ones who read the acclamation. Remember to ask them to do this one too. Make sure the words are listed in your liturgy booklet. And list your choices on the planning sheet.

OPTION 1

Everyone who loves is begotten of God
and knows God. *(1 John 4:7b)*

OPTION 2

God is love.
Let us love another, as God has loved us.
(1 John 4:8b, 11)

OPTION 3

If we love one another,
God remains in us
    and his love is brought to perfection in us.
(1 John 4:12)

OPTION 4

Whoever remains in love,
remains in God and God in him.
(1 John 4:16)

NOTE: This page is reproduced from the Couple's Book.

GOSPEL

In the Gospels, Matthew, Mark, Luke, and John wrote of the saving life and teachings of Jesus Christ. From the selections listed here, select the one that best expresses what you believe as a couple: about your relationship, your love, and the presence of God in your life together. List your selection on the planning sheet. Usually the priest presiding at your wedding reads the Gospel. However, if another priest is concelebrating, he may also be invited to read the Gospel. One further note: usually the person who reads the Gospel also gives a sermon, or homily. Discuss this with the priest as you plan. If a non-Catholic Christian minister is also taking part in the ceremony, he or she may, depending on the regulations of your diocese, proclaim the Gospel and/or deliver the homily. Confer with the priest about this.

OPTION 1

A reading from the Holy Gospel According to Matthew *(5:1–12a)*

When Jesus saw the crowds, he went up the mountain,
    and after he had sat down, his disciples came to him.
He began to teach them, saying:
    "Blessed are the poor in spirit,
        for theirs is the Kingdom of heaven.
    Blessed are they who mourn,
        for they will be comforted.
    Blessed are the meek,
        for they will inherit the land.
    Blessed are they who hunger and thirst
        for righteousness,
        for they will be satisfied.
    Blessed are the merciful,
        for they will be shown mercy.
    Blessed are the clean of heart,
        for they will see God.
    Blessed are the peacemakers,
        for they will be called children of God.
    Blessed are they who are persecuted for the
        sake of righteousness,
        for theirs is the Kingdom of heaven.
    Blessed are you when they insult you
        and persecute you
        and utter every kind of evil against you
        falsely because of me.
Rejoice and be glad,
    for your reward will be great in heaven."

OPTION 2

A reading from the Holy Gospel According to Matthew *(5:13–16)*

Jesus said to his disciples:
"You are the salt of the earth.
But if salt loses its taste, with what
    can it be seasoned?
It is no longer good for anything
    but to be thrown out and trampled underfoot.
You are the light of the world.
A city set on a mountain cannot be hidden.
Nor do they light a lamp and then put it
    under a bushel basket;
    it is set on a lamp stand,
    where it gives light to all in the house.
Just so, your light must shine before others,
    that they may see your good deeds
    and glorify your heavenly Father."

OPTION 3 *[long form]*

A reading from the Holy Gospel According to Matthew *(7:21, 24–29)*

Jesus said to his disciples:
"Not everyone who says to me, 'Lord, Lord,'
    will enter the Kingdom of heaven,
    but only the one who does the will
    of my Father in heaven.

"Everyone who listens to these words of mine
    and acts on them
    will be like a wise man who built his house
    on rock.
The rain fell, the floods came,
    and the winds blew and buffeted the house.
But it did not collapse;
    it had been set solidly on rock.

105

NOTE: This page is reproduced from the Couple's Book.

And everyone who listens to these words of mine
  but does not act on them
    will be like a fool who built his house on sand.
The rain fell, the floods came,
  and the winds blew and buffeted the house.
And it collapsed and was completely ruined."

When Jesus finished these words,
  the crowds were astonished at his teaching,
  for he taught them as one having authority,
  and not as their scribes.

OPTION 3 *[short form]*
A reading from the Holy Gospel
According to Matthew *(7:21, 24–25)*

Jesus said to his disciples:
"Not everyone who says to me, 'Lord, Lord,'
  will enter the Kingdom of heaven,
  but only the one who does the will
    of my Father in heaven.

"Everyone who listens to these words of mine
    and acts on them
  will be like a wise man who built his house
    on rock.
The rain fell, the floods came,
  and the winds blew and buffeted the house.
But it did not collapse;
  it had been set solidly on rock."

OPTION 4
A reading from the Holy Gospel
According to Matthew *(19:3–6)**

Some Pharisees approached Jesus,
    and tested him, saying,
  "Is it lawful for a man to divorce his wife
    for any cause whatever?"
He said in reply, "Have you not read that from
    the beginning
  the Creator *made them male and female* and said,
  *For this reason a man shall leave his father and mother
  and be joined to his wife, and the two shall become
    one flesh?*
So they are no longer two, but one flesh.
Therefore, what God has joined together,
    man must not separate.

OPTION 5
A reading from the Holy Gospel
According to Matthew *(22:35–40)*

One of the Pharisees, a scholar of the law,
    tested Jesus by asking,
  "Teacher, which commandment in the law
    is the greatest?"
He said to him,
  "You shall love the Lord, your God,
  with all your heart,
  with all your soul,
  and with all your mind.
This is the greatest and the first commandment.
The second is like it:
  You shall love your neighbor as yourself.
The whole law and the prophets depend
    on these two commandments."

OPTION 6
A reading from the Holy Gospel
According to Mark *(10:6–9)**

Jesus said:
"From the beginning of creation,
  God made them male and female.
*For this reason a man shall leave his father and mother
  and be joined to his wife,
  and the two shall become one flesh.*
So they are no longer two but one flesh.
Therefore what God has joined together,
  no human being must separate."

NOTE: This page is reproduced from the Couple's Book.

OPTION 7

A reading from the Holy Gospel
According to John *(2:1–11)**

There was a wedding in Cana in Galilee,
    and the mother of Jesus was there.
Jesus and his disciples were also invited
      to the wedding.
When the wine ran short,
    the mother of Jesus said to him,
    "They have no wine."
And Jesus said to her,
    "Woman, why does your concern affect me?
My hour has not yet come."
His mother said to the servers,
    "Do whatever he tells you."
Now there were six stone water jars there
      for Jewish ceremonial washings,
    each holding twenty to thirty gallons.
Jesus told them,
    "Fill the jars with water."
So they filled them to the brim.
Then he told them,
    "Draw some out now and take it
      to the headwaiter."
So they took it.
And when the headwaiter tasted the water
      that had become wine,
    without knowing where it came from
    (although the servants who had drawn the
      water knew),
    the headwaiter called the bridegroom and said
      to him,
    "Everyone serves good wine first,
    and then when people have drunk freely,
      an inferior one;
    but you have kept the good wine until now."
Jesus did this as the beginning of his signs
      in Cana in Galilee
    and so revealed his glory,
    and his disciples began to believe in him.

OPTION 8

A reading from the Holy Gospel
According to John *(15:9–12)*

Jesus said to his disciples:
"As the Father loves me, so I also love you.
Remain in my love.
If you keep my commandments, you will remain
      in my love,
    just as I have kept my Father's commandments
    and remain in his love.

"I have told you this so that my joy might be in you
    and your joy might be complete.
This is my commandment: love one another
    as I love you."

OPTION 9

A reading from the Holy Gospel
According to John *(15:12–16)*

Jesus said to his disciples:
"This is my commandment: love one another
    as I love you.
No one has greater love than this,
    to lay down one's life for one's friends.
You are my friends if you do what I command you.
I no longer call you slaves,
    because a slave does not know what his master is doing.
I have called you friends,
    because I have told you everything
      I have heard from my Father.
It was not you who chose me, but I who chose you
    and appointed you to go and bear fruit
      that will remain,
    so that whatever you ask the Father in my
      name he may give you."

107

NOTE: This page is reproduced from the Couple's Book.

A reading from the Holy Gospel According to John
(17:20–26)

Jesus raised his eyes to heaven and said:
"I pray not only for my disciples,
   but also for those who will believe in me
     through their word,
   so that they may all be one,
   as you, Father, are in me and I in you,
   that they also may be in us,
   that the world may believe that you sent me.
And I have given them the glory you gave me,
   so that they may be one, as we are one,
   I in them and you in me,
   that they may be brought to perfection as one,
   that the world may know that you sent me,
   and that you loved them even as you loved me.
Father, they are your gift to me.
I wish that where I am they also may be with me,
   that they may see my glory that you gave me,
   because you loved me before the foundation
     of the world.
Righteous Father, the world also does not
     know you,
   but I know you, and they know that you sent me.
I made known to them your name and I will
     make it known,
   that the love with which you loved me
   may be in them and I in them."

A reading from the Holy Gospel According to John
(17:20–23)

Jesus raised his eyes to heaven and said:
"Holy Father, I pray not only for these,
   but also for those who will believe in me
     through their word,
   so that they may all be one,
   as you, Father, are in me and I in you,
   that they also may be in us,
   that the world may believe that you sent me.
And I have given them the glory you gave me,
   so that they may be one, as we are one,
   I in them and you in me,
   that they may be brought to perfection as one,
   that the world may know that you sent me,
   and that you loved them even as you loved me."

NOTE: *This page is reproduced from the Couple's Book.*

Rite of Marriage

EXCHANGE OF WEDDING VOWS

INTRODUCTION

Dearly beloved,
you have come together into the house of the Church,
so that in the presence of the Church's minister
   and the community
your intention to enter into Marriage
may be strengthened by the Lord with a sacred seal.
Christ abundantly blesses the love that binds you.
Through a special Sacrament,
he enriches and strengthens
those he has already consecrated by Holy Baptism,
that they may be faithful to each other for ever
and assume all the responsibilities of married life.
And so, in the presence of the Church,
I ask you to state your intentions.

THE QUESTIONS BEFORE THE CONSENT

Priest:
N. and N., have you come here to enter
   into Marriage
without coercion,
freely and wholeheartedly?

Bridegroom and Bride:
I have.

Priest:
Are you prepared, as you follow the path of Marriage,
to love and honor each other
for as long as you both shall live?

Bridegroom and Bride:
I am.

Priest:
Are you prepared to accept children lovingly from God
and to bring them up
according to the law of Christ and his Church?

Bridegroom and Bride:
I am.

THE CONSENT

Priest:
Since it is your intention to enter the covenant
   of Holy Matrimony,
join your right hands and declare your consent
before God and his Church.

OPTION 1
Bridegroom:
I, N., take you, N., to be my wife.
I promise to be faithful to you,
in good times and in bad,
in sickness and in health,
to love you and to honor you
all the days of my life.

Bride:
I, N., take you, N., to be my husband.
I promise to be faithful to you,
in good times and in bad,
in sickness and in health,
to love you and to honor you
all the days of my life.

OPTION 2
Bridegroom:
I, N., take you, N., for my lawful wife,
to have and to hold, from this day forward,
for better, for worse,
for richer, for poorer,
in sickness and in health,
to love and to cherish
until death do us part.

109

NOTE: This page is reproduced from the Couple's Book.

Bride:

I, N., take you, N., for my lawful husband,
to have and to hold, from this day forward,
for better, for worse,
for richer, for poorer,
in sickness and in health,
to love and to cherish
until death do us part.

OPTION 3

Priest:

N., do you take N., to be your wife?
Do you promise to be faithful to her
in good times and in bad,
in sickness and in health,
to love her and to honor her
all the days of your life?

Bridegroom:

I do.

Priest:

N., do you take N., to be your husband?
Do you promise to be faithful to him
in good times and in bad,
in sickness and in health,
to love him and to honor him
all the days of your life?

Bride:

I do.

OPTION 4

Priest:

N., do you take N. for your lawful wife,
to have and to hold, from this day forward,
for better, for worse,
for richer, for poorer,
in sickness and in health,
to love and to cherish
until death do you part?

Bridegroom:

I do.

Priest:

N., do you take N. for your lawful husband,
to have and to hold, from this day forward,
for better, for worse,
for richer, for poorer,
in sickness and in health,
to love and to cherish
until death do you part?

Bride:

I do.

THE RECEPTION OF THE CONSENT

Priest:

OPTION 1

May the Lord in his kindness strengthen the consent
you have declared before the Church,
and graciously bring to fulfillment his blessing within you.
What God joins together, let no one put asunder.

OPTION 2

May the God of Abraham, the God of Isaac, the God of Jacob,
the God who joined together our first parents in paradise,
strengthen and bless in Christ
the consent you have declared before the Church,
so that what God joins together, no one may put asunder.

NOTE: This page is reproduced from the Couple's Book.

BLESSING AND GIVING OF RINGS

Most couples being married today have a two-ring blessing, each giving the other a ring to symbolize their marriage, love, and commitment. When selecting this blessing, read through them carefully, selecting the one that best expresses your love and your hopes. Add this decision to your planning sheet.

OPTION 1

May the Lord bless ✚ these rings,
which you will give to each other
as a sign of love and fidelity.

OPTION 2

Bless, O Lord, these rings,
which we bless ✚ in your name,
so that those who wear them
may remain entirely faithful to each other,
abide in peace and in your will,
and live always in mutual charity.
Through Christ our Lord.

OPTION 3

Bless ✚ and sanctify your servants
in their love, O Lord,
and let these rings, a sign of their faithfulness,
remind them of their love for one another.
Through Christ our Lord.

The husband places his wife's ring on her ring finger, saying, as the circumstances so suggest:

N., receive this ring
as a sign of my love and fidelity.
[optional when marrying a Catechumen or unbaptized person*] In the name of the Father, and of the Son, and of the Holy Spirit.

Likewise, the wife places her husband's ring on his ring finger, saying, as the circumstances so suggest:

N., receive this ring
as a sign of my love and fidelity.
[optional when marrying a Catechumen or unbaptized person*] In the name of the Father, and of the Son, and of the Holy Spirit.

*The rite says "if he or she is a Christian, he/she may add 'In the name of the Father...'" This is not required in a wedding between a Catholic and a Catechumen or unbaptized person. In other words, when both spouses are baptized, the second sentence is always said. However, when a Catholic marries a Catechumen or non-Christian, the second sentence may be added by a spouse who is Christian.

111

NOTE: This page is reproduced from the Couple's Book.

THE *ARRAS* AND THE *LAZO* OR THE VEIL

Many Catholic cultures celebrate the traditions of the Arras, the wedding coins, and the Lazo garland or the veil. In the US, these traditions have now been incorporated into the Order of Celebrating Matrimony as options. Below is how the Order of Matrimony describes these actions. If you wish to celebrate these traditions, be sure to discuss them with the ministers helping you prepare your wedding liturgy.

The Blessing and Giving of the *Arras*

If the occasion so suggests, the rite of blessing and giving of the *arras* (coins) may take place following the blessing and giving of rings.

The Priest says:

Bless, ✢ O Lord, these *arras*
that N. and N. will give to each other
and pour over them the abundance of your good gifts.

The husband takes the arras and hands them over to his wife, saying:

N., receive these *arras* as a pledge of God's blessing
and a sign of the good gifts we will share.

The wife takes the arras and hands them over to the husband, saying:

N., receive these *arras* as a pledge of God's blessing
and a sign of the good gifts we will share.

Then a hymn or canticle of praise may be sung by the whole community.

The Blessing and Placing of the *Lazo* or the Veil

According to local customs, the rite of blessing and imposition of the *lazo* (wedding garland) or of the veil may take place before the Nuptial Blessing. The spouses remain kneeling in their place. If the *lazo* has not been placed earlier, and it is now convenient to do so, it may be placed at this time, or else, a veil is placed over the head of the wife and the shoulders of the husband, thus symbolizing the bond that unites them.

The Priest says:

Bless, ✢ O Lord, this *lazo* (or: this veil),
a symbol of the indissoluble union
that N. and N. have established from this day forward
before you and with your help.

The lazo (or the veil) is held by two family members or friends and is placed over the shoulders of the newly married couple.

112

NOTE: This page is reproduced from the Couple's Book.

UNIVERSAL PRAYER

When writing the petitions, take time to consider what you want to pray for. Most couples will include a prayer for their families, deceased loved ones, other married couples, the church community, world peace, or other particular concerns. Remember to ask the priest if he wants to write his own invitation to pray that begins the prayer, or whether he would like you to write it. Also select a response that you would like said after every petition and list it in your wedding booklet. You will also need to select someone to read these petitions. Make sure that they receive a copy of the petitions in advance to look over them. Here are some examples of petitions given in the Rite of Marriage:

OPTION 1

Dear brothers and sisters,
as we call to mind the special gift of grace and charity
by which God has been pleased to crown and consecrate
the love of our sister N. and our brother N.,
let us commend them to the Lord.

That these faithful Christians, N. and N.,
newly joined in Holy Matrimony,
may always enjoy health and well-being,
let us pray to the Lord.

℟. *Lord, we ask you, hear our prayer.*
(Or another appropriate response of the people.)

That he will bless their covenant
as he chose to sanctify marriage at Cana in Galilee,
let us pray to the Lord. ℟.

That they be granted perfect and fruitful love,
peace and strength,
and that they bear faithful witness to the name of Christian,
let us pray to the Lord. ℟.

That the Christian people
may grow in virtue day by day
and that all who are burdened by any need
may receive the help of grace from above,
let us pray to the Lord. ℟.

That the grace of the Sacrament
will be renewed by the Holy Spirit
in all married persons here present,
let us pray to the Lord. ℟.

Graciously pour out upon this husband and wife, O Lord,
the Spirit of your love,
to make them one heart and one soul,
so that nothing whatever may divide those you have joined
and no harm come to those you have filled with your blessing.
Through Christ our Lord.

℟. Amen.

OPTION 2

Dear brothers and sisters,
let us accompany this new family with our prayers,
that the mutual love of this couple may grow daily
and that God in his kindness
will sustain all families throughout the world.

For this bride and groom,
and for their well-being as a family,
let us pray to the Lord.

℟. *Lord, we ask you, hear our prayer.*
(Or another appropriate response of the people.)

For their relatives and friends,
and for all who have assisted this couple,
let us pray to the Lord. ℟.

For young people preparing to enter Marriage,
and for all whom the Lord is calling to another state in life,
let us pray to the Lord. ℟.

For all families throughout the world
and for lasting peace among all people,
let us pray to the Lord. ℟.

For all members of our families
who have passed from this world,
and for all the departed,
let us pray to the Lord. ℟.

For the Church, the holy People of God,
and for unity among all Christians,
let us pray to the Lord. ℟.

Lord Jesus, who are present in our midst,
as N. and N. seal their union
accept our prayer
and fill us with your Spirit.
Who live and reign for ever and ever.

℟. Amen.

113

NOTE: *This page is reproduced from the Couple's Book.*

Liturgy of the Eucharist

PRAYER OVER THE OFFERINGS

As the priest prepares the bread and wine he offers a prayer over them. This is an appropriate time to offer your new marriage as a gift, asking God to watch over you and protect you. Record your choice on your planning sheet.

OPTION 1

Receive, we pray, O Lord,
the offering made on the occasion
of this sealing of the sacred bond of Marriage,
and, just as your goodness is its origin,
may your providence guide its course.
Through Christ our Lord.

OPTION 2

Receive in your kindness, Lord,
the offerings we bring in gladness before you,
and in your fatherly love
watch over those you have joined in a sacramental covenant.
Through Christ our Lord.

OPTION 3

Show favor to our supplications, O Lord,
and receive with a kindly countenance
the oblations we offer for these your servants,
joined now in a holy covenant,
that through these mysteries
they may be strengthened
in love for one another and for you.
Through Christ our Lord.

NOTE: This page is reproduced from the Couple's Book.

PREFACE

The Preface will only be done if Mass will be celebrated during the ceremony. Each option for the Preface expresses marriage in a different way. Select the one that best fits your relationship, and list it on your planning sheet.

OPTION 1
The dignity of the Marriage covenant

It is truly right and just, our duty and our salvation,
always and everywhere to give you thanks,
Lord, holy Father, almighty and eternal God.

For you have forged the covenant of Marriage
as a sweet yoke of harmony
and an unbreakable bond of peace,
so that the chaste and fruitful love of holy Matrimony
may serve to increase the children you adopt as your own.

By your providence and grace, O Lord,
you accomplish the wonder of this twofold design:
that, while the birth of children brings beauty to the world,
their rebirth in Baptism gives increase to the Church,
through Christ our Lord.

Through him, with the Angels and all the Saints,
we sing the hymn of your praise,
as without end we acclaim:

OPTION 2
The great Sacrament of Matrimony

It is truly right and just, our duty and our salvation,
always and everywhere to give you thanks,
Lord, holy Father, almighty and eternal God,
through Christ our Lord.

For in him you have made a new covenant with your people,
so that, as you have redeemed man and woman
by the mystery of Christ's Death and Resurrection,
so in Christ you might make them partakers of divine nature
and joint heirs with him of heavenly glory.

In the union of husband and wife
you give a sign of Christ's loving gift of grace,
so that the Sacrament we celebrate
might draw us back more deeply
into the wondrous design of your love.

And so, with the Angels and all the Saints,
we praise you, and without end we acclaim:

OPTION 3
Matrimony as a sign of divine love

It is truly right and just, our duty and our salvation,
always and everywhere to give you thanks,
Lord, holy Father, almighty and eternal God.

For you willed that the human race,
created by the gift of your goodness,
should be raised to such high dignity
that in the union of husband and wife
you might bestow a true image of your love.

For those you created out of charity
you call to the law of charity without ceasing
and grant them a share in your eternal charity.

And so, the Sacrament of holy Matrimony,
as the abiding sign of your own love,
consecrates the love of man and woman,
through Christ our Lord.

Through him, with the Angels and all the Saints,
we sing the hymn of your praise,
as without end we acclaim:

115

NOTE: This page is reproduced from the Couple's Book.

NUPTIAL BLESSING

Select the nuptial blessing from the options here that best expresses your understanding of your marriage and your faith in God. List your choice on the planning sheet. Nuptial blessings in weddings where one spouse is a Catechumen or unbaptized person can be found at the end of this section, on page 118.

INTRODUCTION

OPTION 1

Dear brothers and sisters,
let us humbly pray to the Lord
that on these his servants, now married in Christ,
he may mercifully pour out
the blessing of his grace
and make of one heart in love
(by the Sacrament of Christ's Body and Blood)
those he has joined by a holy covenant.

OPTION 2

Now let us humbly invoke God's blessing
upon this bride and groom,
that in his kindness he may favor with his help
those on whom he has bestowed the Sacrament of Matrimony.

OPTION 3

Let us pray to the Lord for this bride and groom,
who come to the altar as they begin their married life,
that (partaking of the Body and Blood of Christ)
they may always be bound together by love for one another.

OPTION 4

Let us humbly invoke by our prayers, dear brothers and sisters,
God's blessing upon this bride and groom,
that in his kindness he may favor with his help
those on whom he has bestowed the Sacrament of Matrimony.

THE BLESSING

OPTION 1

O God, who by your mighty power
created all things out of nothing,
and, when you had set in place
the beginnings of the universe,
formed man and woman in your own image,
making the woman an inseparable helpmate to the man,
that they might no longer be two, but one flesh,
and taught that what you were pleased to make one
must never be divided;

O God, who consecrated the bond of Marriage
by so great a mystery
that in the wedding covenant you foreshadowed
the Sacrament of Christ and his Church;

O God, by whom woman is joined to man
and the companionship they had in the beginning
is endowed with the one blessing
not forfeited by original sin
nor washed away by the flood.

Look now with favor on these your servants,
joined together in Marriage,
who ask to be strengthened by your blessing.
Send down on them the grace of the Holy Spirit
and pour your love into their hearts,
that they may remain faithful in the Marriage covenant.

May the grace of love and peace
abide in your daughter N.,
and let her always follow the example of those holy women
whose praises are sung in the Scriptures.
May her husband entrust his heart to her,
so that, acknowledging her as his equal
and his joint heir to the life of grace,
he may show her due honor
and cherish her always
with the love that Christ has for his Church.

And now, Lord, we implore you:

NOTE: This page is reproduced from the Couple's Book.

may these your servants
hold fast to the faith and keep your commandments;
made one in the flesh,
may they be blameless in all they do;
and with the strength that comes from the Gospel,
may they bear true witness to Christ before all;
(may they be blessed with children,
and prove themselves virtuous parents,
who live to see their children's children).

And grant that,
reaching at last together the fullness of years
for which they hope,
they may come to the life of the blessed
in the Kingdom of Heaven.
Through Christ our Lord.

OPTION 2

Holy Father,
who formed man in your own image,
male and female you created them,
so that as husband and wife, united in body and heart,
they might fulfill their calling in the world;

O God, who, to reveal the great design you formed in your love,
willed that the love of spouses for each other
should foreshadow the covenant you graciously made
    with your people,
so that, by fulfillment of the sacramental sign,
the mystical marriage of Christ with his Church
might become manifest
in the union of husband and wife among your faithful;
Graciously stretch out your right hand
over these your servants (N. and N.), we pray,
and pour into their hearts the power of the Holy Spirit.

Grant, O Lord,
that, as they enter upon this sacramental union,
they may share with one another the gifts of your love
and, by being for each other a sign of your presence,
become one heart and one mind.

May they also sustain, O Lord, by their deeds
the home they are forming
(and prepare their children
to become members of your heavenly household
by raising them in the way of the Gospel).

Graciously crown with your blessings your daughter N.,
so that, by being a good wife (and mother),

she may bring warmth to her home with a love that is pure
and adorn it with welcoming graciousness.

Bestow a heavenly blessing also, O Lord,
on N., your servant,
that he may be a worthy, good and
faithful husband (and a provident father).

Grant, holy Father,
that, desiring to approach your table
as a couple joined in Marriage in your presence,
they may one day have the joy
of taking part in your great banquet in heaven.
Through Christ our Lord.

℟. Amen.

OPTION 3

Holy Father, maker of the whole world,
who created man and woman in your own image
and willed that their union be crowned with your blessing,
we humbly beseech you for these your servants,
who are joined today in the Sacrament of Matrimony.

May your abundant blessing, Lord,
come down upon this bride, N.,
and upon N., her companion for life,
and may the power of your Holy Spirit
set their hearts aflame from on high,
so that, living out together the gift of Matrimony,
they may (adorn their family with children
and) enrich the Church.

In happiness may they praise you, O Lord,
in sorrow may they seek you out;
may they have the joy of your presence
to assist them in their toil,
and know that you are near
to comfort them in their need;
let them pray to you in the holy assembly
and bear witness to you in the world,
and after a happy old age,
together with the circle of friends that surrounds them,
may they come to the Kingdom of Heaven.

Through Christ our Lord.

℟. Amen.

117

NOTE: This page is reproduced from the Couple's Book.

NUPTIAL BLESSING BETWEEN A CATHOLIC AND A CATECHUMEN OR UNBAPTIZED PERSON

Now let us humbly invoke God's blessing
upon this bride and groom,
that in his kindness he may favor with his help
those on whom he has bestowed the bond of Marriage.
(And all pray in silence for a while.)

Holy Father, maker of the whole world,
who created man and woman in your own image
and willed that their union be crowned with your blessing,
we humbly beseech you for these your servants,
who are joined today in the Marriage covenant.
May your abundant blessing, Lord,
come down upon this bride, N.,
and upon N., her companion for life,
and may the power of your Holy Spirit
set their hearts aflame from on high,
so that, living out together the gift of Matrimony,
they may be known for the integrity of their conduct
(and be recognized as virtuous parents).
In happiness may they praise you, O Lord,
in sorrow may they seek you out;
may they have the joy of your presence
to assist them in their toil,
and know that you are near
to comfort them in their need;
and after a happy old age,
together with the circle of friends that surrounds them,
may they come to the Kingdom of Heaven.
Through Christ our Lord.
R. Amen.

If, because of circumstances, the Nuptial Blessing is omitted,
this prayer is spoken over the bride and bridegroom:

Be attentive to our prayers, O Lord,
and in your kindness uphold
what you have established for the increase of the human race,
so that the union you have created
may be kept safe by your assistance.
Through Christ our Lord.
R. Amen.

NOTE: This page is reproduced from the Couple's Book.

PRAYER AFTER COMMUNION

This prayer is used only if Comunion is distributed. Select one of these options and list it on your planning sheet

OPTION 1

By the power of this sacrifice, O Lord,
accompany with your loving favor
what in your providence you have instituted,
so as to make of one heart in love
those you have already joined in this holy union
(and replenished with the one Bread and the one Chalice).
Through Christ our Lord.

OPTION 2

Having been made partakers at your table,
we pray, O Lord,
that those who are united by the Sacrament of Marriage
may always hold fast to you
and proclaim your name to the world.
Through Christ our Lord.

OPTION 3

Grant, we pray, almighty God,
that the power of the Sacrament we have received
may find growth in these your servants
and that the effects of the sacrifice we have offered
may be felt by us all.
Through Christ our Lord.

119

NOTE: This page is reproduced from the Couple's Book.

BLESSINGS AT THE END OF THE CELEBRATION

This blessing is used only when Communion is distributed. The priest offers a prayer for you as your wedding liturgy comes to an end and you are about to embark on your life together as husband and wife. Select the one you want and list it on your planning sheet.

OPTION 1

May God the eternal Father
keep you of one heart in love for one another,
that the peace of Christ may dwell in you
and abide always in your home.
℟. Amen.

May you be blessed in your children,
have solace in your friends
and enjoy true peace with everyone.
℟. Amen.

May you be witnesses in the world to God's charity,
so that the afflicted and needy who have known
    your kindness
may one day receive you thankfully
into the eternal dwelling of God.
℟. Amen.

And may almighty God bless all of you, who are gathered here,
the Father, and the Son, ✠ and the Holy Spirit.
℟. Amen.

OPTION 2

May God the all-powerful Father grant you his joy
and bless you in your children.
℟. Amen.

May the Only Begotten Son of God
stand by you with compassion in good times and in bad.
℟. Amen.

May the Holy Spirit of God
always pour forth his love into your hearts.
℟. Amen.

And may almighty God bless all of you, who are gathered here,
the Father, and the Son, ✠ and the Holy Spirit.
℟. Amen.

OPTION 3

May the Lord Jesus,
who graced the marriage at Cana by his presence,
bless you and your loved ones.
℟. Amen.

May he, who loved the Church to the end,
unceasingly pour his love into your hearts.
℟. Amen.

May the Lord grant
that, bearing witness to faith in his Resurrection,
you may await with joy the blessed hope to come.
℟. Amen.

And may almighty God bless all of you, who are gathered here,
the Father, and the Son, ✠ and the Holy Spirit.
℟. Amen.

120

NOTE: This page is reproduced from the Couple's Book.

Resources

This resource appendix contains an assortment of resources, some of which are hotline numbers for immediate help, and others are for information or referrals. The best way to obtain assistance for yourself or for a loved one is to look for services in your immediate area. Look in your local telephone book or call the Catholic social agency/services number for information. If they are unable to help you, the following list may assist you in reaching help.

One final note: there is nothing here about marriage or family therapy or counseling. We recommend that you seek this locally if you and your partner are experiencing trouble in your relationship. Remember, it's better to seek help early in the problem rather than wait until it's too late.

Al-Anon Family Group Headquarters
888-425-2666
www.al-anon.org

Alcoholics Anonymous
No national phone number. Check local area.
www.alcoholics-anonymous.org

Adult Children of Alcoholics
P.O. Box 3216
Torrance, CA 90510
310-534-1815
www.adultchildren.org

Child Help Hotline
800-422-4453
www.childhelp.org

Cocaine addiction
800-262-2463
800-468-6933
www.cocaineaddiction.com

Co-dependents Anonymous
602-277-7991 (meeting information)
214-340-1777 (to request literature)
http://coda.org

Debtors Anonymous
P.O. Box 920888
Needham, MA 02492
781-453-2743
800-421-2383
www.debtorsanonymous.org

Gamblers Anonymous
No national phone number. Check local area.
International Service Office 213-386-8789

Narcotics Anonymous
818-773-9999
www.na.org

121

NOTE: This page is reproduced from the Couple's Book.

National AIDS Hotline
800-342-AIDS
800-232-4636/CDC info
www.aidshotline.org

National Clearing House for Alcohol and Drug Information
800-729-6686
www.health.gov

National Institute on Drug Abuse
Drug Information and Treatment Referral
301-443-1124
www.nida.nih.gov

Natural Family Planning Office
United States Catholic Conference
3211 4th Street NE
Washington, DC 20017-1194
202-541-3070
www.usccb.org

National Domestic Violence Hotline
800-799-7233
800-787-3224
www.ndvh.org

Overeaters Anonymous
No national phone number. Check local area.
505-891-2664
www.oa.org

Parents Anonymous
No national phone number. Check local area.
909-621-6184
www.parentsanonymous.org

Resolve (infertility support)
703-556-7172
www.resolve.org

Sex Addicts Anonymous
P.O. Box 70949
Houston, TX 77270
800-477-8191
www.sexaa.org
hppt://saa-recovery.org

Sex and Love Addicts Anonymous
1550 NE Loop 410, Ste 118
San Antonio, TX 78209
www.slaafws.org

Sexually Transmitted Disease (STD) Hotline
800-227-8922
CDC 800-311-3435

The Stepfamily Association of America
650 J Street, Suite 205
Lincoln, NE 68508
800-735-0329
www.saafamilies.org

NOTE: This page is reproduced from the Couple's Book.

Happy Together

The Catholic Blueprint for a Loving Marriage
JOHN BOSIO

Every couple hopes to have a happy marriage. Why then do so few reach this goal? Author John Bosio believes that it is only achievable when God and faith are part of the mix. Here he offers couples a blueprint for happiness based on the wisdom of the Christian Tradition. He challenges couples to overcome selfishness by learning to love each other as Christ loves. He identifies and focuses on six key aspects of a loving marriage, and he uses stories and examples to illustrate each. This is a wonderful, open, realistic, and encouraging book about marriage. Highly recommended for married couples, engaged couples, and marriage enrichment groups. This is one of the best new books on Catholic marriage available today!

168 PAGES | $16.95 | 9781585956852

Blessed Is Marriage

A Guide to the Beatitudes for Catholic Couples
JOHN BOSIO

John Bosio draws from his experience as a family therapist and committed believer to provide a path for a loving marriage inspired by the Beatitudes. He offers couples both theological grounding and inspiration as they seek to strengthen their marriage committement.

104 PAGES | $14.95 | 9781585958566

Letters to a Young Married Couple

Practical Wisdom and Guidance
for the Newly Married
KATHY F. HASTY

This beautiful book is a series of short letters written to a newlywed, offering wisdom and practical advice as a way of companioning those starting out on the sacred journey of marriage Through this book, the author's hope is to walk with the reader as a friend, giving reflections in each letter and then inviting the couple to explore each topic further through the discussion questions provided

96 PAGES | $12.95 | 9781627852548

Preparing for a Lifetime of Love

30 Reflections for Engaged Couples
from Pope Francis' The Joy of Love

Drawn from the parts of The Joy of Love in which Pope Francis speaks directly to couples, the thirty brief reflections here help couples remember what is most important about their wedding and marriage—now and throughout their lives together.

32 PAGES | $2.95 | 9781627852333

BOOKLET PRICING

200+ COPIES	$1.49
100-199 COPIES	$1.99
50-99 COPIES	$2.49
1-49 COPIES	$2.95

TO ORDER CALL 1-800-321-0411
OR VISIT WWW.TWENTYTHIRDPUBLICATIONS.COM

TWENTY-THIRD PUBLICATIONS
A division of Bayard, Inc.